English

A* Study Guide
for GCSE and IGCSE

Susan Elkin

GALORE PARK

www.galorepark.co.uk

Published by Galore Park Publishing Ltd
19/21 Sayers Lane, Tenterden, Kent TN30 6BW
www.galorepark.co.uk

Text copyright © Susan Elkin Limited 2010

The right of Susan Elkin to be identified as the author of this Work has been asserted by her in accordance with sections 77 and 78 of the Copyright, Designs and Patents Act 1988.

Design and typography by River Design, Edinburgh
Illustration by Rowan Barnes-Murphy

Printed by Lego S.p.A., Italy

ISBN 978 1 905735 426

All rights reserved: no part of this publication may be reproduced, stored in a retrieval system, or transmitted in any form or by any means, electronic, mechanical, photocopying, recording or otherwise, without either the prior written permission of the copyright owner or a licence permitting restricted copying issued by the Copyright Licensing Agency, Saffron House, 6–10 Kirby Street, London EC1N 8TS

First published 2011

Details of other Galore Park publications are available at www.galorepark.co.uk

ISEB Revision Guides, publications and examination papers may also be obtained from Galore Park.

Photo credits: p. 2 © Aidan Gill/Galore Park Publishing Ltd; p. 4 Frazer Harrison/Getty Images; p. 6 Bull and bear baiting (woodcut) (b&w photo) by English School Private Collection/The Bridgeman Art Library, Nationality/copyright status: English/out of copyright; p. 8 imagebroker/Alamy; p. 11 Jonathan Wood/Getty Images; p. 14 © HarperCollins Publishers Ltd; p. 15 Geraint Lewis/Alamy; p. 18 TongRo Image Stock/Alamy; p. 20 Mary Evans Picture Library/Alamy; p. 29 INTERFOTO/Alamy; p. 33 © Aidan Gill/Galore Park Publishing Ltd; p.34 mauritius images GmbH/Alamy; p. 40 RIA Novosti/Alamy; p. 50 Jon Bower London/Alamy; p. 56 Lebrecht Music and Arts Photo Library/Alamy; p. 58 AF archive/Alamy.

About the author

Susan Elkin MA BA (Hons) Cert Ed taught English for 36 years and was a member of the English department at Benenden from 1993 to 2004. She is now a full-time freelance writer, journalist and author of more than 30 books including *So You Really Want to Learn English* Books 1, 2 and 3 and *English Year 9* published by Galore Park.

Acknowledgements

For Carole Collins-Biggs, my ever supportive sister. With love.

I thank everyone at Galore Park – especially Aidan Gill, Terry Hardy and Ruth Thomas – for all their hard work and skill in developing this book from my raw manuscript. And nothing would happen without the sterling, ongoing support of my husband Nicholas Elkin. Thanks Nick for – among many other things – listening while I (endlessly) bounce ideas and for all that patient, meticulous proof reading.

The publishers are grateful to the following for permission to use the extracts included in this book:

The Closet Thinker: Out of my comfort zone by Justine Picardie is © Telegraph Media Group Limited; extract from *Shakespeare* by Bill Bryson is © 2007 HarperCollins Publishers Ltd; extract from *Cities* © Jan Morris, 1963. Reprinted by permission of A P Watt Ltd on behalf of Jan Morris; extract from *Shadows of the Workhouse* by Jennifer Worth, copyright © Jennifer Worth 2005, published by Weidenfeld & Nicolson, an imprint of The Orion Publishing Group, London; 'What stops us running faster?' from *The Seventy Great Mysteries of the Natural World*, edited by Michael J Benton, is © 2008 Thames & Hudson; extract from *Purple Hibiscus* by Chimamanda Ngozi Adichie is © 2004 HarperCollins Publishers Ltd; *The Christmas Gift* by Hugh Oliver is © the author (permission sought).

Contents

Section Five

Accuracy Section

Spelling Accurately

Introduction

This is not a textbook. It is a guide to help you do your very best and get the highest grade that you can in your GCSE or IGCSE English (and English Literature) assessments.

Its purpose is to help you through your English studies, to remind you of all you have learnt in English lessons and to show you how to write outstanding answers.

How can this book help me?

There are no facts to memorise in English. It is different from subjects like history, geography and science.

English and English Literature assessments test your ability to read perceptively and to write well and accurately as well as giving you the opportunity to show how well you can communicate orally and understand spoken English. In other words, they examine the skills that you have developed over many years through class work.

This book will take you through the various skills that you need, giving examples of excellent answers and providing you with questions so that you can practise what you have learnt.

How is this book organised?

The main body of the book is divided into five sections, as illustrated on the following page. Study tips and examiner's tips appear throughout these sections, while accuracy and spelling are dealt with in two separate sections at the back of the book.

1. Analysing writing: non-fiction

This section explains how to read and respond to factual or discursive material. It includes three examples with notes to show you what you should be looking for and three exercises (one provides an extra challenge) for you to practise your skills.

2. Analysing writing: fiction

This section takes you through an extract from a novel, giving notes on characterisation, dialogue, style, subtext and purpose. There is one exercise based on another short story and another (that provides an extra challenge) based on an extract from a different novel.

3. The spoken word

This section gives advice about how to prepare for speaking and listening tasks and how to write about words spoken by others. Exercises provide opportunities to practise both skills.

4. Your own writing

Whether you are writing prose (to entertain, inform or persuade), poetry, drama or some other form of writing you need to develop interesting, varied and clear ways of expressing yourself. This section gives you advice on how to improve your writing and exercises to practise these skills.

5. Writing about literature

This section shows you how to shape and express your responses to the novels, stories, plays and poems you have studied. It also shows you how to compare one text with another and gives an example of an empathy essay.

Study tips and examiner's tips

These tips, which give you hints on how to prepare for your assessments and exams and how to impress the examiner, appear throughout the book. Using these tips will help you to improve your grade and could take your work to A* level. There is also a separate page of A* tips (see page IX), with reminders throughout the book to refer you back to them.

Achieving A* through accuracy

The penultimate section provides a useful summary of the main points of grammar and punctuation. It also includes a list of ten mistakes to avoid if you want your writing to be A* level.

Spellings

Spelling is very important indeed. It underpins everything you write and is linked closely to accuracy. Therefore the book concludes with the words that are most likely to give you problems.

How will I be assessed?

Part of your GCSE assessment will consist of formal exam papers. The rest will involve controlled assessments – written work done in the classroom under a teacher's supervision and then sent off to external assessors. Speaking and listening assignments are assessed mostly by teachers in your own school. The work in this book relates to both forms of assessment.

If you are entered for IGCSE English all the assessment for written work rests on exam papers.

English

There are five examination boards (OCR, Edexcel, AQA, WJEC and CCEA) setting GCSE examinations in England, Wales and Northern Ireland. IGCSE is examined by Edexcel and CIE (Cambridge International Examinations). Although the details of what is tested by which method and what goes in which exam paper vary from one board to another, the basic material is the same for all.

All boards have four assessment objectives (AOs) which successful GCSE and IGCSE English candidates must meet. They are:

AO1: Speaking and listening
AO2: Study of spoken language

AO3: Studying written language
AO4: Writing

All GCSE and IGCSE English courses and assessments consist of combinations of these aspects of the subject.

You cannot really separate English from English Literature since all literature consists of language and language can only be studied by looking at what has been written or spoken in it. That is why these complementary subjects are often taught in the same lessons.

English Literature

Although all GCSE and IGCSE English courses include some study of literature (Shakespeare, for example) you may also be taking English Literature as an additional subject. In most schools the two are taught together as part of the same course and some boards allow you to study some of the same books for both subjects. The AOs for English Literature can be summarised as:

AO1: Critical and imaginative reading
AO2: Writers' methods

AO3: Comparison of texts
AO4: Background

Remember that there are almost as many ways of approaching a novel, short story, poem or play as there are readers. This is not maths and there are no right or absolute answers – only the responses of intelligent and perceptive readers (that's you) who can support their ideas with evidence from the text.

Susan Elkin, December 2010

Additional resources

In order to supply specific practice for the different examination boards, there are practice exam papers at www.EnglishAStar.com, which have been produced by Susan Elkin. They are not past papers but follow the format of the exam board they each relate to, thereby offering invaluable exam-based practice and revision.

A* tips

This book is all about achieving A*, so here is a list of tips to bear in mind when studying and revising for your GCSE and IGCSE assessments. Throughout the book you will find this symbol, which acts as a prompt to look back at this page and remind yourself of these tips to A* success.

General points for achieving A*
- Always read the question carefully, several times
- Answer the question fully, or do whatever the task asks you to do
- Express your ideas or a particular viewpoint clearly and concisely, in good English, whether written or spoken
- Write or speak clearly with precision and in an appropriate tone
- Use a wide vocabulary, accurately and appropriately, whether speaking or writing
- Spell and punctuate accurately
- Adapt language for different purposes
- Use language to persuade others to a point of view
- Convey information orally with clarity
- Consider the writer's perspective: what the writer does, how the effect is achieved, why it is done, what is the effect on the audience

Analysing writing: non-fiction and fiction
- Construct a clear argument or line of reasoning
- Make good use of frequent and relevant short quotations within your sentences

The spoken word
- Understand the use of different registers and styles for different purposes (such as the difference, for example, between a role play between a drug pusher and teenager in a club, someone complaining about faulty goods in a shop, making a formal presentation)
- Make appropriate use of techniques such as rhetoric
- Show an ability to use spoken language to entertain
- Listen accurately to others and respond orally in an appropriate way
- Demonstrate the ability to absorb and adapt the speech of others

Writing: your own and about literature
- Demonstrate the ability to absorb and adapt the writing of others
- Understand the use of different styles for different purposes

Section One

1 Analysing writing: non-fiction

At some point in your GCSE or IGCSE assessments and exams you will be required to write about passages and texts in an analytical way.

Some of the passages and texts you will be analysing will be non-fiction and some will be fiction.

Depending upon which examination board you are using, you may have to analyse some of the following:

- material taken from texts you have studied over several months in class
- pre-release material that is shown to you shortly before an assessment
- unseen material that is completely new to you and which you will have to work on without help
- spoken material such as podcasts (see Section 3).

In many cases the same texts also serve as a basis, or starting point, for your own writing, which we will look at in Section 4.

In this chapter we will look at some of the ways in which you might approach the written material you are expected to analyse.

Non-fiction texts can include:

- biography
- autobiography
- history
- travel
- science
- newspaper, magazine or website articles about almost anything
- book, theatre and other reviews.

Study TIP The key things to remember are that you should:

- become a critical reader
- take nothing at face value
- read between the lines.

It is a very wide category and includes almost every kind of writing except fiction (stories, poems or plays which someone has made up).

When you are tackling a non-fiction text, you should ask yourself five main questions:

1. What is the **genre** of this text? Is it, for example, autobiographical, stating an opinion, arguing a case, humour, travel, scientific, social history, informative? State somewhere in your response the genre of the text you are analysing.
2. What is distinctive or interesting about the writer's **style** (the use of language)?
3. What is his or her **purpose** in writing this piece?
4. What is he or she telling the reader indirectly? (What is the **subtext**?)
5. Who is the piece written for? (Who is the **audience**?)
6. Does it work in this format or would it have been better presented differently? (How effective is the **presentation**?)

Note

The **subtext** in a piece of writing is what lies behind or beneath the words, the hidden agenda or 'what the text says but does not say' as the French philosopher Jacques Derrida (1930–2004) put it. Some people now call the subtext of a piece of writing – or other sort of text – its **perspective**.

Your first task when faced with a passage is to read it several times. Once you have read it through for meaning and general impression, look at it more closely with the questions above in mind.

Let us consider the three contrasting non-fiction passages on the following pages. They are in order: 'The Closet Thinker' by Justine Picardie, from the *Sunday Telegraph*, *Stella* magazine; an extract from *Shakespeare* by Bill Bryson and an extract from 'La Paz' by Jan Morris. After each are some points relating to the questions you should be asking yourself. Their purpose is to show you the sorts of things that you, as a critical reader, should be looking for. In each case, however, these are only starting-point notes. There is much more that could be said and written.

At the end of the three passages there are two exercises and 'An extra challenge' exercise for practice in analysing non-fiction texts.

Study TIP

It may help you to make notes (in pencil) in the margin and/or underline or highlight anything that strikes you as important in relation to the questions you are using to focus your response.

'The closet thinker' by Justine Picardie, *Stella, Sunday Telegraph* (10 January 2010)

Anyone who lives with teenage sons, as I do, will be familiar with the sight of boys in baggy tracksuit bottoms, worn low enough to reveal boxer shorts beneath. It therefore demands a giant leap of faith to give any credence to the news that sweatpants have been deemed the height of cutting-edge fashion; as seen on Agyness Deyn and in designer collections by Isabel Marant, Alexander Wang, DKNY and Helmut Lang.

It's not that I object to them in principle – at this time of year, they're perfect to wear while lolling around indoors, contemplating a gentle stroll to the park – but the idea of accessorising them with a pair of high heels and a tailored blazer (as seen on the aforementioned catwalks) seems utterly ludicrous. The whole point of tracksuit bottoms – or rather, sweatpants, in 21st century transatlantic parlance, although it's an utterly ghastly word – is that they're as cosy as a pair of pyjamas. You don't go out in them, unless you're actually about to engage in some form of sporting activity, or feeling overtired, under-appreciated, and somewhat depressed. As Jerry says to George in *Seinfeld*: 'You know the message you're sending out to the world with these sweatpants? You're telling the world, "I give up. I can't compete in normal society. I'm miserable, so I might as well be comfortable."'

> nothing is more likely to reveal the abyss of the generation gap than seeing fortysomethings hanging out in low-hanging, dropped-crotch tracksuit bottoms, especially with a designer label

Obviously, this is not the case if you see a muscular hip-hop star or a basketball champion or a premier-league footballer. And teenagers can get away with them, too, just like they get away with other sartorial mismatches (yellow tights with denim shorts, black leather biker boots with pink miniskirts); plus, if anyone can make baggy bottoms look desirably cool, it's a pert teenage girl. Which is possibly why grown-ups who should be old enough to know better are intent on proving that they can still keep up with the kids (yet more evidence of the remorseless march of the kidult consumers).

Personally I think nothing is more likely to reveal the abyss of the generation gap than seeing fortysomethings hanging out in low-hanging, dropped-crotch tracksuit bottoms, especially with a designer label attached. In their dreams they're strolling along the beach in Malibu in soft cotton sweatpants, golden skinned, well toned, and barefoot in the sand; in reality, it's a British January, and we've all got bags under our eyes and look like pale mushrooms in the darkness.

I would therefore suggest a late New Year's resolution, which is keep tracksuits in their proper place: on the sofa, naturally…

Style

Picardie uses the first person ('as I do' and 'It's not that I object'), which makes it clear that she is expressing a personal view. She also addresses her imagined reader directly ('if you are a muscular hip-hop star') which gives the piece directness, although this is also a device to express her views about what people should and shouldn't do.

She uses a blend of quite formal educated vocabulary ('credence', 'ludicrous', 'parlance', 'aforementioned') and homely images, such as 'cosy as a pair of pyjamas' and 'bags under our eyes'. The contrast contributes to the lightly humorous tone of the piece.

The humour is highlighted by the imaginative use of alliteration to add to the ridicule ('baggy bottoms'), imaginative and apt imagery ('pale mushrooms in the darkness') and the dreamy use of holiday brochure language ('strolling along the beach in Malibu in soft cotton sweatpants, golden skinned, well toned, and barefoot in the sand') to make her target sound even sillier.

Her style is assertive. She ridicules the idea of trying to look dressed up in tracksuit bottoms or sweatpants. And she thinks middle-aged people wearing these 'low-hanging, dropped-crotch' garments other than to sit at home on their own sofas will look very out of touch.

Picardie deliberately writes in a mildly snobbish style, condemning 'sweatpants' as an 'utterly ghastly word' and carefully choosing the word sofa rather than 'settee'. On the other hand, she breaks grammar conventions for effect to make her writing sound modern, not too fussy and perhaps 'cool'. She writes for example 'just like they get away with' instead of 'just as' and she begins a part sentence after a semi-colon with the popular word 'plus'.

Purpose

Picardie, whose main purpose is to entertain, dislikes, or is pretending for the purpose of this article to dislike, tracksuit bottoms on older wearers and wants to share her views via a fashion column in the magazine section of a broadsheet Sunday newspaper.

She is writing for mainly female readers (few men want to read about clothes and fashion), most of whom will be educated to the same sort of vocabulary levels. Picardie is also appealing to their prejudices. Few of her readers will be teenagers and many of the older women readers of the *Sunday Telegraph* will regard tracksuit bottoms as scruffy and 'common' so they will nod in agreement with Picardie and buy the newspaper again next week.

She mentions several fashion designers and the American TV sit-com *Seinfeld* to show that she is aware of what is going on around her. She walks a fine line between styling herself as an 'old fogey' and presenting herself as being casually and effortlessly up to date with a flattering assumption that the reader is too.

Subtext

Picardie is suggesting to the reader that she is in her forties ('teenage sons') and a sensible family woman with whom readers can reasonably identify. She is interested in fashion – she names several quite classy, less than obvious designers – but is also a person who likes 'lolling around indoors' watching TV programmes such as *Seinfeld* from her sofa.

She also conveys, without stating it overtly, an amused tolerance of teenagers and their ways. For example, she seems to have a sneaking admiration for the 'pert teenage girl' who just might (Picardie is not definite about it) be able to 'make baggy bottoms look desirably cool'.

Audience

This is a woman in her forties writing for an adult readership. She expects her readers to identify with her as the mother of teenage sons in their 'baggy tracksuit bottoms' and to agree with her, adult to adult, that such fashions are fine for the young or on someone very fit doing sport but that they are inappropriate for older people to be seen out in. This is clearly a fashion column aimed at women. Even the title of the magazine, 'Stella', is unlikely to attract men.

Presentation

Picardie is using a distinctive voice and vocabulary to make her point. Although this piece is illustrated with a visual image of someone wearing tracksuit trousers it is not dependent on this. It could equally well have been presented orally as a podcast or radio talk. It would have added Picardie's physical voice to the message which might have made it even more forceful. On the other hand, the list of fashion designers she mentions is probably more easily absorbed when written than it would have been spoken.

From *Shakespeare* by Bill Bryson (2007)

William Shakespeare could not have chosen a more propitious moment to come of age. By the time he arrived in London in (presumably) the late 1580s, theatres dotted the outskirts and would continue to rise throughout his career. All were compelled to reside in 'liberties', areas mostly outside London's walls where City laws and regulations did not apply. It was a banishment they shared with brothels, prisons, gunpowder stores, unconsecrated graveyards, lunatic asylums (the notorious Bedlam stood close by the Theatre) and noisome enterprises like soapmaking, dyeing and tanning – and these could be noisome indeed. Gluemakers and soapmakers rendered copious volumes of bones and animal fat, filling the air with a cloying smell that could be all but worn, while tanners steeped their products in vats of dog faeces to make them supple. No one reached a playhouse without encountering a good deal of odour.

> a bear was put in a ring, sometimes tethered to a stake, and set upon by mastiffs

The new theatres did not prosper equally. Within three years of its opening, the Curtain was being used for fencing bouts, and all other London playhouses, with the single eventual exception of the Globe, relied on entertainments, particularly animal baiting, to fortify their earnings. The pastime was not unique to England, but it was regarded as an English speciality. Queen Elizabeth often had visitors from abroad entertained with bear baiting at Whitehall. In its classic form, a bear was put in a ring, sometimes tethered to a stake, and set upon by mastiffs; but bears were expensive investments, so other animals (such as bulls and horses) were commonly substituted. One variation was to put a chimpanzee on the back of a horse and let the dogs go for both together. The sight of a screeching ape clinging for dear life to a bucking horse while dogs leapt at it from below was considered about as rich an amusement as public life could offer. That an audience that could be moved to tears one day by a performance of *Doctor Faustus* could return the next to the same space and be just as entertained by the frantic deaths of helpless animals may say as much about the age as any single statement could.

Style

Bryson rarely writes more than a few lines without humour even when he is writing about something quite serious. For example, in the opening sentence he pretends that Shakespeare had a choice about his own birth and when he came of age. In the sentence which begins 'It was a banishment …' he makes humour out of the incongruity of gunpowder stores, unconsecrated graveyards, soap-making businesses and the rest being categorised with theatres for their nuisance level.

The use of a number of quite short, often grammatically simple, sentences ('The new theatres did not prosper equally.' and 'Queen Elizabeth often had visitors from abroad entertained with bear baiting at Whitehall.') make this a smooth and accessible passage to read.

Because he is writing about the 16th century, Bryson drops in an occasional slightly unusual, arguably old-fashioned, word such as 'noisome' instead of 'noisy' and 'fortify' instead of 'increase'. This adds to the gentle, witty tone of the writing. Although the piece is easy to read, Bryson favours adult, educated and very precise vocabulary with word choices such as 'propitious', 'copious' and 'prosper'.

Bryson's style is very direct. He doesn't attempt to be polite about, or use euphemisms to describe, the 'products in vats of dog faeces' or the 'screeching ape clinging for dear life to a bucking horse while dogs leapt at it from below'.

Purpose

Bryson is writing to inform and there are a lot of facts in this passage. In this respect Passage 2 is different from Passage 1, the main purpose of which was to entertain. Bryson is entertaining too, but that is secondary. Here we learn about the new theatres in the 1580s, where they were built and why, as well as the sort of entertainments that were presented in them.

This passage is taken from a book called *Shakespeare* so we assume that this is a tiny fragment and that the brief reference to Shakespeare at the beginning will soon lead to something more about him. In a sense, this little passage is probably a digression to set the scene so the reader knows what London was like (even how it smelled!) at the time when Shakespeare is thought to have arrived there.

Subtext

We learn quite a lot about Bryson in this passage from things that he makes clear without stating overtly. For example, he is an educated and bookish sort of chap – and implicitly assumes that the reader who has picked up a book about Shakespeare is too – who finds it quite amusing that in the 16th century, theatres, now regarded as hubs of culture, were lumped together with lunatic asylums, brothels and smelly tanning businesses.

He also conveys a horrified, enlightened 21st century attitude to animal welfare, commenting with very effective understatement that chimpanzee- and horse-baiting 'was considered about as rich an amusement as public life could offer'. He then expresses unstated astonishment (and expects the reader to agree) that Elizabethan theatregoers could apparently 'be moved to tears one day' by one of the profoundest plays of the era and enjoy 'the frantic deaths of helpless animals' twenty-four hours later. The subtext creates an impression of a very humane writer.

Audience

Bryson is writing for people who, like him, have an eclectic curiosity about what happened in the past and how it connects with the present. This is an extract from a full-length book so it assumes that the reader who has bought or borrowed it is as interested in Shakespeare and his times as Bryson is. His is a very enthusiastic style which invites the reader to come on an informative, congenial and witty fact-finding journey. Bill Bryson has an enormous following and the intended audience for this book would partly be people who have read and enjoyed his earlier books. So, there's a sense in the writing of the reader spending time in the good company of an old friend.

Presentation

This is relaxed, educated writing with a fairly complex, though always accessible, vocabulary. There is a strong sense of the author's voice coming through in the informal style. Therefore this would probably work just as well if it were read aloud because none of the sentences is over long. It would add another dimension to the already clear impact of Bryson's voice.

Note

An audio CD of *Shakespeare* read by the author is available as an alternative, or supplement, to reading the book. Bryson and his publishers evidently agreed with the above. And it could be that Bryson knew all along that it would also be recorded and had this in mind as he wrote.

From 'La Paz' by Jan Morris, taken from *Cities* (1963)

Southwards from the glistening steel-blue Titicaca runs the highway through the Bolivian altiplano, leaving the Peruvian highlands behind. To the east stand the splendours of the Andean cordillera, rank upon rank of noble snow-peaks, but the road passes through a landscape more lunar than celestial, an arid, drear, friendless kind of country, fourteen thousand feet above the sea. It is littered with the poor mud huts of the Aymara Indians, and the piles of stones they have scraped and scrabbled from their miserable soil, and sometimes you meet a peasant with his donkeys or his llamas, and sometimes you set the dust flying in an adobe village, and sometimes you see far away across the wilderness some solitary Indian woman, like a huddled witch on a moor, hastening bent-back across the rubble.

For sixty miles the road plods on through this monotony, and then it falls over a precipice. Suddenly it crosses the lip of the high plateau and tumbles helter-skelter, lickety-split into a chasm: and as you slither down the horseshoe

> sometimes you see far away across the wilderness some solitary Indian woman, like a huddled witch on a moor, hastening bent-back across the rubble

bends you see in the ravine below you, secreted in a fold of the massif, the city of La Paz. Its red roofs and mud huts pile up against the canyon walls and spill away into the river valley below. All around it is the immensity of the altiplano, and high above it to the south meditates the lovely white mountain called Illimani, where the royal condor of Inca legend folded its great wings in sleep. La Paz is the highest of the world's big cities, at twelve thousand feet. It is a tumultuous, feverish, often maddening, generally harum-scarum kind of place: but nobody with an eye to country or a taste for drama could fail to respond to its excitements, or resist the superb improbability of its situation.

Style

This is a first person account of a journey through Bolivia in South America but Morris uses 'you' rather than 'I'. When she says that 'sometimes you set the dust flying' or 'as you slither down' she means that she did.

The style is breathless and excited with a large number of adjectives, often in lists, to convey the wonder of what the author is seeing and describing: 'glistening, steel-blue'; 'arid, drear, friendless'; 'tumultuous, feverish, often maddening, generally harum-scarum'.

Morris's longish, unfolding sentences reflect the way the sights are appearing before her eyes. When the road suddenly descends after 60 miles on flat ground she sees La Paz, 'the highest of the world's big cities'. The sentence in which she first sees the city accelerates in pace so that the reader shares the sensation: 'Suddenly it crosses the lip of the high plateau and tumbles helter-skelter, lickety-split into a chasm: and as you slither down the horseshoe bends you see in the ravine below you, secreted in a fold of the massif, the city of La Paz.' The reader is held in suspense through seven subordinate phrases and clauses, until the climax of the sentence, which comes in the last two words. The writing is a carefully paced, dramatic narrative.

Morris's style is also noteworthy for its strong and very apt verbs such as 'littered', 'crosses', 'scraped' and 'scrabbled'.

Her use of rhyming or assonant compound adverbs and adjectives such as 'helter-skelter', 'lickety-split' and 'harum-scarum' contributes to the excited rhythm of the piece.

She uses very carefully chosen images to convey a sense of place and atmosphere: the lone Indian woman is 'like a huddled witch on a moor'; the landscape is 'lunar'; the huts in the city 'pile up' against the canyon walls and 'spill away' into the valley.

Purpose

This is a piece of travel writing. Its main aim is to convey to the reader who hasn't been there a vivid sense of what it feels and looks like to approach La Paz by road.

Like all travel writers, Morris is entertaining as well as informing her readers, few of whom will ever make the journey that she has. The reading is a substitute for the experience.

Subtext

Although she doesn't say it outright, we are led to assume from this passage that Jan Morris has sympathy for the Bolivian poor in their 'poor mud huts' and 'miserable soil'. She does not, however, write about them sentimentally. Adjectives such as 'poor' and 'miserable' make the facts clear enough.

Morris is herself, we infer, the kind of person who has 'an eye to country' and 'a taste for drama' which is why she is responding with this colourful writing to the 'excitements' and 'superb improbability' of La Paz, twelve thousand feet above sea level.

We also deduce that Morris is well versed in the history and culture of the area she is visiting and describing. She knows the myths that relate to Mount Illimani.

Audience

Morris is describing La Paz as graphically, vividly and imaginatively as she can so that 'armchair travellers' can share the experience with her. She is opening doors for people who are not such intrepid travellers as she is and will probably not go to these places themselves.

Presentation

Morris paints three-dimensional pictures in words and adds sound so effectively here that it's hard to imagine how a different presentational format could have improved this piece. Had it been presented, for example, as a TV travel documentary, viewers would have seen more, but there would have been less of Morris's rich interpretation to enhance the viewer's experience, because documentaries usually use more visual effects and fewer words. The written format enables her to be colourful and expressive.

Exercise 1

Read this non-fiction passage several times. Make notes under the five headings: style, purpose, subtext, audience and presentation.

Then use your notes to answer this question:

• **What do you find interesting about this passage?**

Mr Collett

A fire was burning merrily in the hearth and a hod of coal stood beside it. I noticed a tin bath full of coal under the sink. A very beautiful grandfather clock stood proudly against the opposite wall, next to a large wooden crate full of sticks and old newspapers. A heavy wooden table – the sort antique dealers would fight over today – filled the centre of the room, and some grimy plates and mugs were spread out on a newspaper. The room was full of old military photographs, prints and maps, and what looked like medals and trophies, yellowed with age and dirt. I concluded that Mr Collett had been a soldier.

> The stench was revolting, and I felt the nausea rising as I struggled to peel off the layers of bandages, which were stuck to each other with slimy fluid

Our patient sat down in a high wooden chair next to the fire, took his slippers off and placed his right foot on a low stool. He pulled up his trouser leg, revealing horrible blood-and-pus soaked bandages. Sister Julienne told me to do the dressing, whilst she watched me. I knew everything had to be disposed of in the patient's house, so I placed newspapers on the wooden floor. I kneeled down and started to undo the bandages with forceps.

The stench was revolting, and I felt the nausea rising as I struggled to peel off the layers of bandages, which were stuck to each other with slimy fluid. I let them fall onto the newspaper to be burned on the fire. The ulcer was the worst I had ever seen, extending upward from the ankle for about six to eight inches. It was deep and suppurating badly. I cleaned it with saline, packed the cavities with gauze soaked in flavine, and rebandaged. Then the other leg had to be treated.

Mr Collett didn't complain while I was attending to his legs, but sat back sucking an old pipe with no tobacco in it, talking now and then to Sister Julienne. The grandfather clock ticked loudly, and the fire crackled and blazed. The siren of a cargo boat echoed through the room as I completed the second dressing and bandaged up the leg, with the quiet satisfaction of knowing that I had made this dignified old soldier more comfortable.

From *Shadows of the Workhouse* by Jennifer Worth (2005)

Worth was a district nurse and midwife during the 1950s, working in London's desperately poor East End.

Exercise 2

Read this non-fiction passage several times. Make notes under the five headings: style, purpose, subtext, audience and presentation.

Then use your notes to answer this question:

- How effective is this passage?

What stops us running faster?

The difference between fast and very fast running, whether looking at an individual or comparing average to elite sprinters, is most apparent in the forces experienced by the legs: high sprint speeds require high leg forces. If the forces along the legs are increased by requiring a sprinter to go round a tight, but banked, bend, foot timing adjusts to spread the load across a longer stance; this, however, also leads to the slowing of the athlete. Indoor 200m sprint results can be successfully predicted from outdoor results by taking into account the increased forces due to running around bends.

> When racing, these dogs hit speeds around 64 km per hour (40 miles per hour), and they are able to maintain these speeds when sprinting around the bends on the track

Surprisingly, the same does not apply to galloping greyhounds. When racing, these dogs hit speeds around 64 km per hour (40 miles per hour), and they are able to maintain these speeds when sprinting around the bends

on the track. What is more, centrifugal forces effectively increase the greyhound's weight by 71% on the bend, and yet are not adequately compensated for by increasing the time each foot spends on the ground. As a result, the legs experience an average force on the bend of 165% of that on the straight. It appears therefore that maximum speed in greyhounds is not force-limited, and it remains a mystery why they cannot run faster along the straight.

From *The Seventy Great Mysteries of the Natural World* edited by Michael J Benton (2008)

An extra challenge ...

Read this passage carefully several times. It is more demanding than the previous ones and working on it should help to take you to – and beyond – that coveted A*.

Make notes on its style, purpose, subtext, audience and presentation.

Then write a full and thorough answer to this question:

- **What do you find interesting in Gibbon's writing here?**

A candid but rational inquiry into the progress and establishment of Christianity may be considered as a very essential part of the history of the Roman Empire. While that great body was invaded by open violence, or undermined by slow decay, a pure and humble religion gently insinuated itself into the minds of men, grew up in silence and obscurity, derived new vigour from opposition, and finally erected the triumphant banner of the cross on the ruins of the Capitol. Nor was the influence of Christianity confined to the period or to the limits of the Roman empire. After a revolution of thirteen or fourteen centuries, that religion is still professed by the nations of Europe, the most distinguished portion of human kind in arts and learning as well as in arms. By the industry and zeal of the Europeans it has been widely diffused to the most distant shores of Asia and Africa; and by the means of their colonies has been firmly established from Canada to Chile, in a world unknown to the ancients.

But this inquiry, however useful or entertaining, is attended with two peculiar difficulties. The scanty and suspicious materials of ecclesiastical history seldom enable us to dispel the dark cloud that hangs over the first age of the church. The great law of impartiality too often obliges us to reveal the imperfections of the uninspired teachers and believers of the gospel; and, to a careless observer, *their* faults may seem to cast a shade on the faith which they professed. But the scandal of the pious Christian, and the fallacious triumph of the Infidel, should cease as soon as they recollect not only *by whom*, but likewise *to whom*, the Divine Revelation was given. The theologian may indulge the pleasing task of describing Religion as she descended from Heaven, arrayed in her native purity. A more melancholy duty is imposed on the historian. He must discover the inevitable mixture of error and corruption which she contracted in a long residence upon earth, among a weak and degenerate race of human beings.

From *Decline and Fall of the Roman Empire*, Edward Gibbon, Volume 1, 1776

Section Two

Analysing writing: fiction

Reading a fiction text critically and analytically requires some of the same skills that you need to apply to non-fiction texts and some additional ones.

These skills are dealt with fairly briefly here as we come back to them in Section 5, Writing about Literature, which covers the skills needed for GCSE and IGCSE English Literature.

Here is a checklist of five questions to ask yourself as you read fiction for your GCSE or IGCSE English assessments:

1. What is interesting about his or her writing **style**?
2. What is the writer trying to tell the reader indirectly? (**subtext**)
3. Does this writing have a **purpose** other than to entertain?
4. How does the writer bring his or her characters to life? (**characterisation**)
5. What use does the writer make of **dialogue** and how effective is it?

Bear in mind, however, that fiction writers do not set out to write neat stories because they want their work to be GCSE texts! Authors write creatively and in any way they wish. These five areas will always overlap – often messily. Using these headings is simply of way of helping you to make sure that you look at, and write about, all aspects of the text.

Let us consider a fiction passage taken from *Purple Hibiscus* by Chimamanda Ngozi Adichie. After the passage, there are some points that demonstrate the sorts of things that you, as a critical reader, should be looking for.

At the end of the passage there is an exercise and 'An extra challenge' exercise for practice in analysing fiction.

> **Note**
> Chimamanda Ngozi Adichie lived for several
> years in the USA where *Purple Hibiscus*, her first
> novel, was originally published. It therefore uses
> American spellings: 'molded', 'Anglicized', 'color'
> and so on.

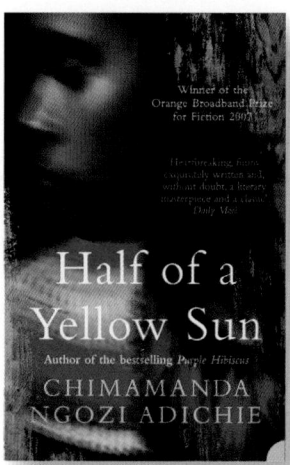
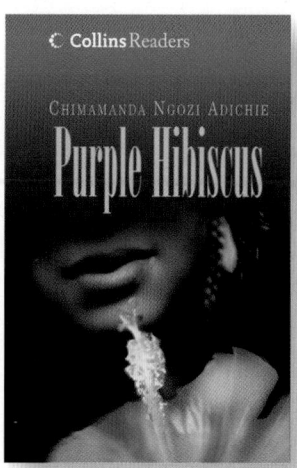

This passage comes from *Purple Hibiscus*, a novel by Chimamanda Ngozi Adichie (2004). The narrator Kambili and her brother Jaja have been brought up as strict Christians in a prosperous Nigerian household. Here they are briefly allowed to visit their grandfather who is relatively poor, still worships the traditional African gods and is disapproved of by certain members of his family.

Papa-Nnukwu was sitting on a low stool on the verandah, bowls of food on a raffia mat before him. He rose as we came in. A wrapper was slung across his body and tied behind his neck, over a once white singlet now browned by age and yellowed at the armpits.

'*Neke! Neke! Neke!* Kambili and Jaja have come to greet their old father!' he said. Although he was stooped with age, it was easy to see how tall he had once been. He shook Jaja's hand and hugged me. I pressed myself to him just for a moment longer, gently, holding my breath because of the strong, unpleasant smell of cassava that clung to him.

> His lower lip quivered,
> as did his voice

'Come and eat,' he said, gesturing to the raffia mat. The enamel bowls contained flaky fufu and watery soup bereft of chunks of fish or meat. It was custom to ask, but Papa-Nnukwu expected us to say no – his eyes twinkled with mischief.

'No, thank sir,' we said. We sat on the wood bench next to him. I leaned back and rested my head on the wooden window shutters, which had parallel openings running across them.

'I hear that you came in yesterday,' he said. His lower lip quivered, as did his voice, and sometimes I understood him a moment or two after he spoke because his dialect was ancient; his speech had none of the anglicized inflections that ours had.

> the age spots that dotted his hand
> stood out because they were so
> much lighter than his soil-colored
> complexion

'Yes,' Jaja said.

'Kambili, you are so grown up now, a ripe *agbogho*. Soon the suitors will start to come,' he said, teasing. His left eye was going blind and was covered by a film the color and consistency of diluted milk. I smiled as he stretched out to pat my shoulder; the age spots that dotted his hand stood out because they were so much lighter than his soil-colored complexion.

'Papa-Nnukwu, are you well? How is your body?' Jaja asked.

Papa-Nnukwu shrugged as if to say there was a lot that was wrong but he had no choice. 'I am well, my son. What can an old man do but be well until he joins his ancestors?' He paused to mold a lump of fufu with his fingers. I watched him, the smile on his face, the easy way he threw the molded morsel out toward the garden, where parched herbs swayed in the light breeze, asking Ani, the god of the land, to eat with him.

'My legs ache often. Your Aunty Ifeoma brings me medicine when she can put the money together. But I am an old man; if it is not my legs that ache, it will be my hands.'

'Will Aunty Ifeoma and her children come back this year?' I asked.

Papa-Nnukwu scratched at the stubborn white tufts that clung to his bald head. '*Ehye*, I expect them tomorrow.'

'They did not come last year,' Jaja said.

'Ifeoma could not afford it.' Papa-Nnukwu shook his head. 'Since the father of her children died, she has seen hard times. But she will bring them this year. You will see them. It is not right that you don't know them well, your cousins. It is not right.'

Jaja and I said nothing. We did not know Aunty Ifeoma or her children very well because she and Papa had quarrelled about Papa-Nnukwu. Mama had told us. Aunty Ifeoma stopped speaking to Papa after he barred Papa-Nnukwu from coming to his house, and a few years passed before they finally started speaking to each other.

'If I had meat in my soup,' Papa-Nnukwu said, 'I would offer it to you.'

'It's all right, Papa-Nnukwu,' Jaja said.

Papa-Nnukwu took his time swallowing his food. I watched the food slide down his throat, struggling to get past his sagging Adam's apple, which pushed out his neck like a wrinkled nut. There was no drink beside him, not even water. 'That child that helps me, Chinyelu, will come in soon. I will send her to go and buy soft drinks for you two, from Inchie's shop', he said.

> the shrine at the corner of the yard, where Papa-Nnukwu's god was, where Papa said Jaja and I were never to go near

'No, Papa-Nnukwu. Thank sir,' said Jaja.

'*Ezi okwu*? I know your father will not let you eat here because I offer my food to our ancestors, but soft drinks also? Do I not buy that from the store as everyone else does?'

'Papa-Nnukwu, we just ate before we came here,' Jaja said. 'If we're thirsty, we will drink in your house.'

Papa-Nnukwu smiled. His teeth were yellowed and widely spaced because of the many he had lost. 'You have spoken well my son. You are my father, Ogbuefi Olioke, come back. He spoke with wisdom.'

I stared at the fufu on the enamel plate, which was chipped of its leaf-green color at the edges. I imagined the fufu, dried to crusts by the harmattan winds, scratching the inside of Papa-Nnukwu's throat as he swallowed. Jaja nudged me. But I did not want to leave; I wanted to stay so that if the fufu clung to Papa-Nnukwu's throat and choked him, I could run and get him water. I did not know where the water was, though. Jaja nudged me again and I still could not get up. The bench held me back, sucked me in. I watched a gray rooster walk into the shrine at the corner of the yard, where Papa-Nnukwu's god was, where Papa said Jaja and I were never to go near. The shrine was a low, open shed, its mud roof and walls covered with dried palm fronds. It looked like the grotto behind St Agnes, the one dedicated to Our Lady of Lourdes.

'Let us go, Papa-Nnukwu.' Jaja said, finally rising.

'All right my son,' Papa-Nnukwu said. He did not say 'What, so soon?' or 'Does my house chase you away?' He was used to our leaving moments after we arrived. When he walked us to the car, balancing on his crooked walking stick made from a tree branch, Kevin came out of the car and greeted him, then handed him a slim wad of cash.

'Oh? Thank Eugene for me,' Papa-Nnukwu said, smiling. 'Thank him.'

He waved as we drove off.

Style

Adichie uses a mixture of dialogue and Kambili's silent observations and recollections (she is looking back from some point in the future) to tell her story. Many of the sentences are short and grammatically simple: 'He shook Jaja's hand and hugged me', 'Jaja and I said nothing', 'Mama had told us' and 'Jaja nudged me', which heightens the poignancy of the children's being so uncomfortable with their grandfather. Papa-Nnukwu speaks very simply and directly too: 'My legs ache often', 'It is not right'.

Kambili's thoughts are often more complex and troubled which is mirrored in the less direct language in which her inner world is expressed: 'I watched him, the smile on his face, the easy way he threw the molded morsel out toward the garden, where parched herbs swayed on the light breeze, asking Ani, the god of the land, to eat with him.' There is a hint here of something which is almost envy. Kambili is silently impressed by Papa-Nnukwu's comfortable manner despite his poverty.

Adichie's style incorporates some interesting and appropriate imagery such as likening Papa-Nnukwu's near-blind eye to the 'color and consistency of diluted milk' and his adam's apple to a 'wrinkled nut'. It is homely and gentle and adds to the sense of Kambili's tenderness towards her grandfather.

Purpose

Adichie is exploring the effects on traditional Nigerian life of the ways of the white man who colonised the country and brought Christianity. One of the things the colonisation caused was rifts in families when some members adopted the 'new' ways very rigidly. She is also showing that family tensions are universal. The setting for this passage happens to be Nigeria but families everywhere have disagreements, so part of Adichie's purpose is to stress the universality of some of the situation she depicts here.

Subtext

Although this passage is, on the surface, an account of two children visiting and talking to their grandfather, there is a great deal simmering just below the surface. Adichie, through Kambili, tells us that Papa-Nnukwu is not welcome in his rich son's house. We also learn that Papa, the children's father, has issued them with many orders about their behaviour which they meekly obey, even when they are under pressure to do otherwise and they are not being allowed to act normally.

Papa's sister Ifeoma is different, we infer. She quarrelled with her brother about Papa-Nnukwu whom she visits when she can and buys medicine for when possible. This is Adichie's way of showing that there is more than one way for an educated African to treat a 'traditionalist' parent.

At base, this passage is about the conflict between the traditional Nigerian ways – epitomised by Papa-Nnukwu and his shrine – and the Christian ways practised at the Church of St Agnes. The profound irony is that the former reminds Kambili of the latter so there isn't really all that much difference between the two attitudes to life.

Characterisation

There are four characters 'present' in this passage: Papa-Nnukwu, Kambili, Jaja and, at the end, Kevin the family chauffeur. But Adichie also hints at the characters of three other people who are in Kambili's thoughts and memory rather than physically present on Papa-Nnukwu's verandah: Papa, Mama and Aunty Ifeoma.

Adichie shows us Kambili being inwardly troubled and ambivalent. She notices Papa-Nnukwu's poverty (the dirty singlet, basic food and his smell), presumably because this is very different from what she's used to. She feels uncomfortable because she and her brother are strictly forbidden ('I know your father will not let you eat here') to accept hospitality from their grandfather and yet she feels very tender towards him. She notices his age (the cataract in his eye, age spots on his hands, bald head and 'crooked walking stick') and is afraid that he might choke on his food when he's alone. Although she says very little aloud she is presented as thoughtful and imaginative, worrying about lumps of fufu sticking in the old man's throat and comparing the shrine in Papa-Nnukwu's yard with one in a church.

Jaja, presented here by Adichie through Kambili, is more confident than his sister. He does nearly all the talking and is scrupulously, formally polite to the old man – which tells the reader more about his rigid upbringing.

Papa-Nnukwu is intelligent and perceptive. Adichie has Kambili tell us that 'his eyes twinkled with mischief' and that he teased her about her grown-up body. He understands exactly the position that the children are in and isn't surprised when they leave very soon after their arrival. We see a stoical, cheerful man – who is grateful for the money his son has sent via the chauffeur. He is much more relaxed than either of his grandchildren.

Indirectly, Adichie shows us that Papa, the children's father and Papa-Nnukwu's son, is a strict man who has rejected his ancestor-worshipping father – apart from allowing his children to make a fifteen-minute annual visit and coldly sending money via the chauffeur. He has forbidden the children to accept food or drink from their grandfather or to go near the shrine in his yard. His widowed sister, Ifeoma, the children's aunt, on the other hand, visits the old man when she can and was estranged from her brother for a long time because of his attitude to their father. The children know this because their mother – one step removed from the quarrel – has told them about it.

Dialogue

Adichie makes it clear that the dialogue in this passage is taking place in an African language (actually Igbo – the most widespread of Nigeria's three main cultures/languages) which Papa-Nnukwu speaks in a way the children with their 'Anglicized inflections' are not used to: 'His dialect was ancient'. It means Kambili has to listen very carefully: '… sometimes I understood him a moment or two after he spoke'.

The children ask their grandfather rather formal questions 'Papa-Nnukwu, are you well? How is your body?' and 'Will Aunty Ifeoma and her children come back this year?'. The old man answers these questions quite naturally and informally; the children's answers to his questions are very stilted and guarded.

Exercise 3

Read the story below very carefully several times. Hugh Oliver is a Canadian author who wrote this story in 1986.

Now make notes on it under the headings style, purpose, subtext, characterisation and dialogue.

The Christmas Gift

It was Christmas Eve. All day it had been snowing – thick flakes that piled against the doors and covered the fields with a carpet of white. And in one of the lonely farmhouses on the Canadian prairie, a child was being born.

The child's father, John, paced the floor of the living-room. He was anxious. It was now three hours since his wife Jessie had begun to give birth. This was to be their first child. They were both old, and they had wanted a child for a long time.

> he was surprised, almost fearful, to find on the step a man he had never seen before

'I wish that the doctor had been able to come,' thought John. 'If only the snow hadn't been so deep. But what am I worrying about? It happens to thousands every day. And Jessie's mother is up there with her.'

Outside in the darkness, everything was silent except for the gentle pattering of snow flakes on the window and the trees creaking beneath their icy loads. As John sat in front of the wood fire, he heard a knock at the door. Imagining it might perhaps be the doctor, he was surprised, almost fearful, to find on the step a man he had never seen before.

'Will you give me shelter?' asked the stranger.

John hesitated. But seeing the stranger's sad appearance – snow blanketing his coat and even clinging to his hair – he invited him in. He helped him off with his coat, and said that he could spend the rest of the night in front of the

fire. He gave the stranger food to eat, and the man was grateful.

'Why are you out on a snowy night like this?' asked John.

'I have much to do,' said the stranger. 'And I have far to go.'

'But where are you going?' asked John.

'In this world,' said the stranger, 'I go wherever they will welcome me.'

John thought him odd, but questioned him no more. The stranger warmed himself in silence for a while in front of the fire.

Then John told him that his wife Jessie was at that moment giving birth to their first child in the room above.

> He stood holding the child, and his silence was his sorrow

'I know,' said the stranger.

'How can you know?' asked John.

'I heard her cry out,' he said.

But John had heard no sound.

The child was born at two o'clock in the morning. It was born dead. Jessie fell into an exhausted sleep. Her mother put the dead child into the cradle beside her. Then she went downstairs to tell John what had happened.

John was numb with despair. When he looked at the table spread with all the good things for Christmas, there was no joy in him any more.

'What was it?' he asked.

'A boy,' said Jessie's mother. 'Would you like to see him?'

'I would,' answered John. 'Then I'll take him away. I shouldn't like Jessie to see him – not dead.'

John went upstairs and looked lovingly at his sleeping wife. He was thankful that she had not been taken from him as well.

He gazed at the pathetic little body in the cradle. Then he lifted it out and carried it downstairs.

He stood holding the child, and his silence was his sorrow.

'He was not dead,' said the stranger 'He had never lived'

The stranger asked if he might take the child. Saying nothing, John gave it to him. The stranger rocked the child in his arms and kissed the child's forehead.

'Why do you do that?' asked Jessie's mother. 'The child is dead.'

'He needs to be made warm,' said the stranger.

'But he's dead,' repeated Jessie's mother.

The stranger smiled and continued to rock the child.

And John watching saw the child's eyes open, and Jessie's mother listening heard the child cry out.

'Why you have done a miracle,' shouted John. 'You have brought the child back from death.'

'He was not dead,' said the stranger. 'He had never lived.'

He gave the child to Jessie's mother. 'Quickly!' he said. 'Take him upstairs to his mother before she wakes.' He turned to John.

'And now,' he said 'I must be on my way.'

John did not know what to do – to laugh for joy or to weep

John stood at the door, watching the stranger until he was out of sight

for joy, to kiss the stranger or what to do. 'You must stay,' he said. 'You must stay with us for ever.' But the stranger stood at the door putting on his coat.

'At least stay for Christmas,' pleaded John. 'Look I have all these good things.' He pointed to the table. 'And you who have made our happiness should share it.'

But the stranger would not stay. Thanking John for his kindness, he opened the door and walked out across the snow.

It had stopped snowing. John stood at the door, watching the stranger until he was out of sight. Then, as he turned to go indoors, he was filled with wonder; for he saw that where the stranger had walked, there were no footprints in the snow.

An extra challenge ...

This passage is more demanding than anything you are likely to be presented with at GCSE. So use it as a way of further developing your A* skills.

Read it carefully several times and make notes on style, subtext, purpose, characterisation and dialogue before you undertake this task:

• **Write a detailed analysis of this passage.**

In this extract from Thomas Hardy's 1896 novel *Jude the Obscure*, Jude a countryman who longs to study at Oxford (which Hardy calls Christminster) arrives at the city.

He now paused at the top of a crooked and gentle declivity, and obtained his first near view of the city. Grey stoned and dun-roofed, it stood within hail of the Wessex border, and almost with the tip of one small toe within it, at the northern-most point of the crinkled line along which the leisurely Thames strokes the fields of that ancient kingdom. The buildings now lay quiet in the sunset, a vane here and there on their many spires and domes, giving sparkle to a picture of sober secondary and tertiary hues.

Reaching the bottom he moved along the level way between pollard willows growing indistinct in the twilight, and soon confronted the outmost lamps of the town – some of those lamps which had sent into the sky the gleam and glory that caught his strained gaze in his days of dreaming, so many years ago. They winked their yellow eyes at him dubiously, and as if, though they had been awaiting him all these years in disappointment at his tarrying, they did not much want him now.

He was a species of Dick Whittington whose spirit was touched to finer issues than a mere material gain. He went along the outlying streets with the cautious tread of an explorer. He saw nothing of the real city in the suburbs on this side. His first want being a lodging he scrutinised carefully such localities as seemed to offer on inexpensive terms the modest type of accommodation he demanded; and after inquiry took a room in a suburb nick-named 'Beershaba', though he did not know this at the time. Here he installed himself, and having had some tea sallied forth.

It was a windy, whispering, moonless night. To guide himself he opened under a lamp a map he had brought. The breeze ruffled and fluttered it but he could see enough to decide on the direction he should take to reach the heart of the place.

After many turnings he came up to the first ancient mediaeval pile that he had encountered. It was a college,

as he could see by the gateway. He entered it, walked round and penetrated to dark corners which no lamplight reached. Close to this college was another; and a little further on another: and then he began to be encircled as it were with the breath and sentiment of the venerable city. When he passed objects out of harmony with its general expression he allowed his eyes to slip over them as if he did not see them.

A bell began clanging, and he listened till a hundred-and-one strokes had sounded. He must have made a mistake, he thought: it was meant for a hundred.

When the gates were shut, and he could no longer get into the quadrangles, he rambled under the walls and doorways, feeling with his fingers the contours of their mouldings and carving.

Section Three

Human beings communicated with each other by speaking long before they developed ways of writing. Even today we use speech far more than we use writing – most of us speak many more words every day than we write.

This form of communication is a two-way process. If one person is speaking then someone else (or more than one person) is listening.

The spoken word has two separate strands:

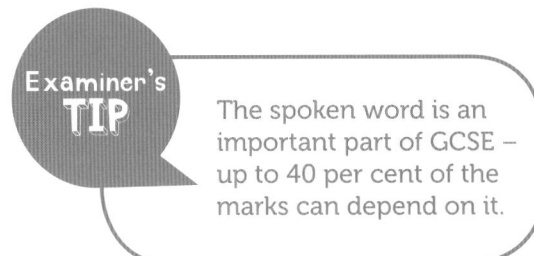

Examiner's **TIP**

The spoken word is an important part of GCSE – up to 40 per cent of the marks can depend on it.

- practical speaking and listening tasks on which you are assessed internally (by your teacher who sends the marks to the examination board) – often known as oral work
- studying words spoken, for instance, on radio, podcasts, in speeches, in plays or elsewhere, and writing about them in an analytical way.

In some cases you will have the opportunity to listen to recordings of the spoken word before you write your analysis under controlled classroom conditions.

Instead, or in addition, you may be required to read a written transcript of the spoken word and write about it in an exam. This may feel a bit strange since you have to pretend that you can 'hear' something that is, in fact, written.

All candidates undertake the same sorts of oral assignment, but A* candidates will distinguish themselves by learning, remembering and utilising the techniques listed as A* tips on page IX.

Speaking and listening tasks

Your speaking and listening skills will probably be assessed three times and in three different ways. The details will vary according to the examination board that you are using, but you could be expected, for example, to prepare:

- a presentation in which you tell the group about something that interests you or express a point of view persuasively
- a group discussion in which you listen to each other's views and respond
- a drama assignment – such as a role play – working individually, in a pair or in a small group, in which you pretend to be someone else, using appropriate language.

Choosing topics

- If your teacher allows you a free choice of discussion topic, consider choosing something relating to one of the books you have read in connection with the rest of English or English Literature GCSE or IGCSE (for example, 'Is Macbeth evil or is he misled?' or 'What is Wilfred Owen trying to tell us in "Dulce et decorum est"?'). Preparing for your oral assessment will then help with your other revision.

- For a role play or a drama-focused oral task, use the books you are studying too (for example, you might role-play an imagined, but appropriate, dialogue between Pip and Estella in *Great Expectations* or Mr and Mrs Bennett in *Pride and Prejudice*. Or you could work on a rehearsed reading of a section of *Death of a Salesman*, *An Inspector Calls*, or whatever play(s) you are studying). Again, it is a way of making your revision work in more than one way.

Preparation

- For an individual assessment, write brief notes on cards small enough to hold in the palm of your hand. Do not write out what you intend to say in full and then read it.

- For a discussion with others, talk about the topic in general terms first but don't over rehearse or try to script it. Discussion is, by its very nature, meant to be spontaneous. Your job is to show not that you know everything there is to know about the subject – or that your views are the 'right' ones – but that you can contribute in a reasoned way and that you can listen and respond to what others say.

Delivery

- Make as much eye contact with your listeners as you can.

- If you are using notes on cards, turn the card over once you have covered what is written on it.

- Think about body language and the impression you are giving. Stand square on two feet (this is not the moment to play storks!), relax your shoulders and try to look self assured. If you can look confident then you are more likely to feel confident. This is what actors do all the time.

Examiner's **TIP**

Use some of these phrases in your discussion assessments:

- On the other hand …
- Well, I hear what you're saying but …
- That's true but …
- I don't agree. I …
- I can go along with three-quarters of what you say but I must take issue with you about …
- I don't think we're going to agree on this …
- What do you think about …?
- Does anybody else agree …?
- Have you considered …?
- Shouldn't we ask ourselves …?

Features of the spoken word

The following features tend to be more common in speech than in written material:

pauses which are unmarked by punctuation. Few speakers deliver their words as smoothly as writers. Actors deliberately do this in dialogue in plays to make the words sound spontaneous and conversational. Giggles, coughs, sighs and so on sometimes fill these pauses.	
filler words such as 'well', 'er', 'umm' and many others. These are partly thinking time for the speaker and partly an indication of informality. (You may also notice that many politicians and other interviewees on TV begin their answers with 'That's a very interesting question' or something similar to give themselves time to think.)	'Hello, umm, everyone. My, er, presentation is about, er, how to speak fluently and without too much, umm, hesitation.'

- **half sentences, phrases and other fragments** used as if they were full sentences. Writers do this too, especially if they want to sound informal.

'A belief in society. Working together. Solidarity. Cooperation. Partnership. These are our words ...'
Tony Blair to Labour Party Conference in Blackpool (1994)

'Your joy for life transmitted wherever you took your smile and the sparkle in those unforgettable eyes. Your boundless energy which you could barely contain.'
Earl Spencer at the funeral of his sister Diana, Princess of Wales (1997)

Note the use of phrases rather than sentences in both cases.

- **unfinished sentences.**

- **interruptions** when there is more than one speaker as in, for example, an interview.

- **colloquial language** if it's casual speech. (You wouldn't expect the Prime Minister at Prime Minister's Question Time to declare him – or her – self 'cool' with a decision but it would seem very ordinary if you heard it said by someone on a bus.)

- **formal language** – even high-flown or pompous language – if it's an important speech by someone eminent speaking to a large audience.

'Today, all of us do, by our presence here, and by our celebrations in other parts of the country and the world, confer hope and glory to newborn liberty.'
Nelson Mandela upon release in 1994 after 27 years in prison

'Nineteen ninety two is not a year I shall look back on with undiluted pleasure.'
HM Queen Elizabeth II (1992)

Note the formal language – vocabulary and sentence structure – in both cases.

Study TIP

Listen to as many examples of the spoken word as you can, listening carefully for, and making notes on, examples of the above features.

Good sources of spoken word material include:

- radio, such as the *Today* programme, Monday to Saturday mornings on Radio 4
- podcasts of programmes, talks, etc.
- TV programmes such as *Question Time* on BBC1
- recordings of plays
- speeches made anywhere (school assemblies, weddings, funerals, sermons, public expressions of thanks, politicians on TV, charity appeals, eavesdropping on public transport, etc.)

Exercise 4

The following is an example of a written transcript, taken from a BBC recording of a conversation between Bush and Blair.

Read the transcript carefully several times and then complete the following tasks:

- Make notes on the language used in this dialogue. Pay particular attention to the ways in which it differs from written language.
- Explain why there are these differences. Think about the effect of the speakers being able to see each other and communicate in other ways, for example.
- How do you think this conversation might have continued? Write a few more lines in the same style.
- Using the same transcript format write a short, imaginary, informal conversation between two people of your choice who happen to be in a unusual situation.

A transcript of an off-the-cuff conversation between US President George W Bush and UK Prime Minister Tony Blair during a break at the G8 conference in Russia in 2006. By chance it was picked up by a microphone and recorded.

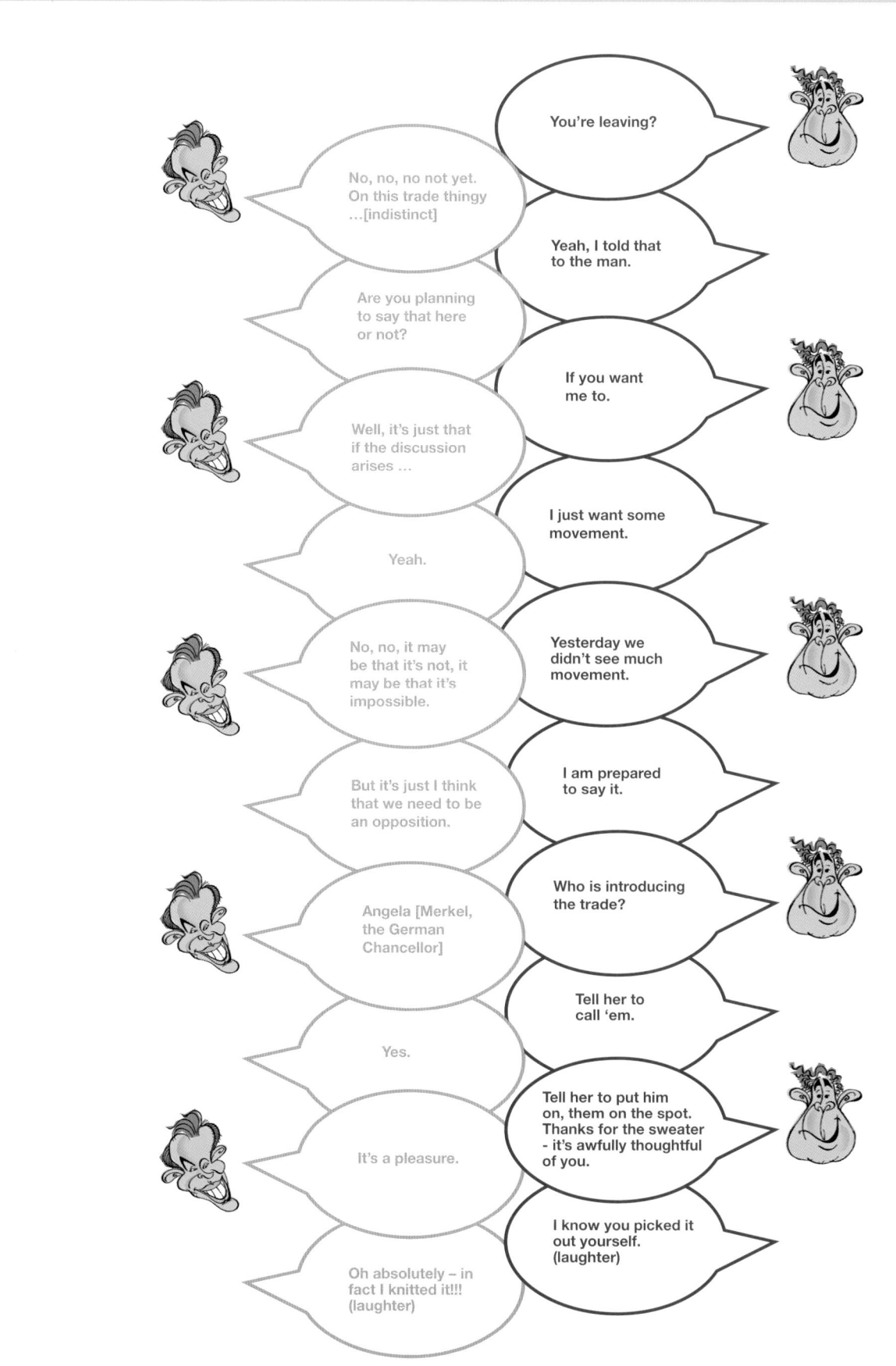

extract from *Transcript: Bush and Blair's unguarded chat*, from the BBC News website (18 July 2006),
© bbc.co.uk/news 2006

Rhetoric

Rhetoric is the art of using speech to persuade, influence or please.

Skilled rhetoricians often use several easily recognisable techniques which it is worth listening out for and commenting on.

These include:

- **repetition**

  In 1963 Martin Luther King made a passionate speech, which became very famous, about racial equality. In it he repeats the word 'Now' (stressed) three times. He quotes the line 'Let freedom ring,' which comes from a hymn, nine times. Most famously of all he says 'I have a dream …' nine times. It is a very effective and memorable way of conveying a point. Read and/or hear the whole speech at www.americanrhetoric.com/speeches/mlkihaveadream.htm

- **lists of three**

  It is worth noting that Martin Luther King used both three or nine repetitions – three groups of three. He didn't use twos, fours or eights. Another American politician Edward Kennedy said in a speech in 1988 of two people who had been assassinated: 'But they left us their vision, their values and the hopes they awakened' – a rhetorical triplet. Another example is St Paul declaring to the Corinthians 'And now abideth faith, hope and charity, these three; but the greatest of these three is charity.'

- **rhetorical questions**

  These are questions to which the answer is self-evident. If a headteacher stands in assembly and says 'Do we really want this school to win the cup on Saturday?' she isn't expecting an answer. She assumes that every listener will agree with her that yes, we all want the school to win the cup. Such questions are often asked for dramatic effect.

'For us, they packed up their few worldly possessions and travelled across oceans in search of a new life.
For us, they toiled in sweatshops and settled in the West; endured the lash of the whip and ploughed the hard earth.
For us, they fought and died, in places like Concord and Gettysburg; Normandy and Khe Sahn.'
President Barack Obama (January 2009)

Note both the use of repetition and lists of three in the three repetitions of 'For us, they …' in these three sentences.

'Hath not a Jew eyes?
Hath not a Jew hands, organs, dimensions, senses, affections, passions?
If you prick us, do we not bleed, if you tickle us, do we not laugh?
If you poison us, do we not die?'
Shylock in William Shakespeare's The Merchant of Venice

Notice the use of rhetorical questions and repetition.

Exercise 5

Look up Mark Antony's funeral speech for Caesar in *Julius Caesar* (Act 3, scene 2, line 75), which begins 'Friends, Romans, countrymen' (another rhetorical triplet).

This is an example of a skilled rhetorician in a play. Shakespeare has given Antony these words to speak to show the audience what is going on in Antony's mind and how he works when he is addressing the public.

Count the number of times he says 'Brutus is an honourable man' and work out what he actually wants his listeners to conclude.

Read the speech again and complete the following tasks:

- Make a list of the rhetorical devices which Shakespeare has Mark Antony use and make notes on their effectiveness and impact.
- If you were directing this scene – as part of a play – in performance, how would you stage it to maximise the effect of the rhetoric?

Section Four

4   Your own writing

At some point during your GCSE or IGCSE assessment you will be expected to produce some original writing of your own.

It could be, for example:

- fiction – a story or part of one
- writing to inform – such as a travel article or advice about how to organise a meal for four guests
- writing to persuade – in which you try to convince your reader that, for instance, the age for driving licence eligibility should be lowered to sixteen
- a play script or part of one
- poetry
- a speech to persuade or inform
- a news article for a newspaper or magazine
- a letter, formal or informal, but with a purpose – perhaps to complain about faulty goods or to describe an event
- a memoir – an account of something that has happened to you or that you have seen or experienced
- a review of a book, play, film or restaurant
- a description of something from your own experience such as a place or person you know
- fictional descriptive writing in which you write colourfully and imaginatively about a place, person or thing of your own invention.

Of course, this is not an exhaustive list. There are plenty of other things that you might be asked, or choose, to write about.

Such writing is referred to by teachers and examiners as creative, personal, individual or imaginative writing. Some people prefer the traditional word 'composition', a loose, umbrella term that covers any sort of writing.

Sometimes the writing you are set to do is (loosely) related to a text you have been given to read and asked to respond to in some other way first (see Sections 1 and 2).

You could, for example, be asked to read a newspaper article about something controversial (such as the punishment of underage offenders or the hunting ban) and write a letter to the newspaper commenting on the issue and expressing your views.

Alternatively, you may be asked to read something and present it in some other format. For example, you could be given a transcript of a journalist's interview with someone, written like a play text, and be asked to write that journalist's article for his or her newspaper or magazine.

You could be asked to write a review of a fiction text you have been studying, or asked to expand the story of a minor character in a familiar set text or play.

You will do your writing as a controlled assessment (in class under a teacher's supervision, usually with plenty of time) or in a formal examination in which your time will be strictly limited. The detailed arrangements for when you write and how long you are allowed will vary according to the examination board you are using.

Exercise 6

IGCSE candidates in 2008 were asked to choose one of these six tasks (a–f) and to write 350–400 words. Use any, some or all of these to practise your writing skills.

Argumentative/discursive writing

a) Write the words of a speech entitled 'Basic rights for teenagers'. In your speech your aim should be to persuade both young people and adults to consider your views.

b) 'Travel broadens the mind.' Is this statement still true in the era of the internet, which can tell us every thing about any country and its people at the tap of a key?

Descriptive writing

c) Describe a time when you were waiting for something unpleasant or fearful to happen. Describe the place where you were at the time and your feelings as you waited … and waited.

d) The sounds of laughter and loud voices attract your attention to a room in your house. The door is closed. Describe what you can hear, as well as what you can see, as you gently open the door.

Narrative writing

e) 'The figure sprinted away from the angry crowd and headed towards a gap between the buildings.' Use this sentence to start a story.

f) As you shake your morning breakfast cereal from the box, out tumbles a small, red envelope with the words 'Open me now!' stamped on it. Inside, there is a list of instructions that you must carry out 'before night falls'. Write the story of your day.

Study TIP

Practise your response skills by reading closely as many articles in newspapers and magazines and on websites as you can. Then set yourself some sort of responsive task.

Exercise 7

Read the following abridged version of an article, which appeared in the *Daily Mail* in 2006.

Then write one of the following:

- **a dialogue between two teenagers discussing this article in the form of a play text**
- **two or three letters expressing contrasting points of view for publication in the newspaper**
- **a first person account by the American girl in the lift of her encounter with this British journalist and what the girl really thought.**

Can you think of any other way of responding to this piece in writing?

'Hello, I've just had my nails done – do you like them?' said a girl aged about 13 – a complete stranger – looking at me squarely in the eye with calm confidence. She then told me about the salon she'd been to and why she'd chosen it.

Of course we weren't in Britain. She and I were in a hotel lift in Montgomery, Alabama.

It was an interesting example of everyday oral communication by someone who knew how to instigate and sustain a chatty conversation. Intellectual? No. Pleasingly communicative? Yes.

You hear it all round you in US streets and diners wherever you go. Poised young people talk comfortably to each other and to adults. It's quite a recommendation for the American education system.

Listen, for comparison, to the youth of Britain as it swarms along our streets – if you can bear to. Someone once dubbed their speech 'communication by grunt' and that's a fairly polite description of the consonantless stream of diphthongs I hear from far too many. It's a big contrast to the smiling American clarity which predominates on the streets of New York or Los Angeles.

In Britain the only word which is clearly enunciated occurs at least once in every 'sentence': the emotive one which begins with 'f'.

It's dire enough when you hear them spilling out of the school gates. The loud and incomprehensible gurglings as they leave the pubs on a Friday or Saturday after an evening of under-age drinking are worse still.

When speaking to adults many British school children are hesitant and indistinct. Bellowing at each other and muttering at adults seems to be the norm.

Any young man or woman of say, 14, jolly well ought to be able to look **anyone** in the eye and to speak in a straightforward manner which can be understood by both parties. But few can unless, apparently, they're American.

This country has got itself into a dreadful muddle with oral communication. What used to be described as 'well spoken' is now ungrammatically condemned as 'talking posh'. The use of clear diction and the ability to say confidently what you mean is frequently sneered at. And it's certainly not taught in most schools.

Whether you're packing in a factory, working in an office or serving the public, more than 80% of all communication is oral not written. So shortcomings on spoken English are very serious.

Perhaps we should find out how they teach oral communication in America – and fast.

Daily Mail, Susan Elkin, 2006

Exercise 8

Practise your argumentative/discursive **writing skills with some of these ideas:**

- Many children and teenagers are overweight and some are developing illnesses as a result of this. What has caused the 'obesity crisis' and what can be done about it? Write a newspaper article in which you try to persuade young people and adults to your point of view.
- Should adults be permitted to smoke in the presence of children? Write the words of a speech arguing your case.
- The 19th century poet Alfred Lord Tennyson wrote that

    ''tis better to have loved and lost
    Than never to have loved at all.'

    Was he right? Think about friendships and other relationships breaking up or about relationships that end with the death of either partner and write your answer.

Exercise 9

Practise your descriptive **writing skills with some of these ideas:**

- Describe a place you know well at two contrasting times – at night and during the day, when it is quiet and when it is very busy, in summer and in winter, or choose other circumstances that change the place's atmosphere. The place you choose could be a street, station, building, open space or anything else you wish.
- Write a description of a person – his/her appearance, habits, way of speaking, manner, place he/she is associated with. Be selective with the details you include and make it as lively and vivid as possible. It could be a real person known to you or an invention.
- You witness a serious and quite complex road accident. Describe exactly what happened as clearly as you can.
- What is your earliest memory? Write about it, including as many interesting and colourful details as you can.

Exercise 10

Practise your narrative **writing skills with some of these ideas:**

- Write a story called 'Falling'.
- Write a story that begins with the sentence 'It all began because Clare's granny came to stay ...'.
- 'We knew we were in trouble as soon as we saw that large black car gliding menacingly towards us.' Continue this story.

Improving your writing

Whether you are writing an argumentative, descriptive or narrative piece there are certain aspects of your writing that you can work on in order to improve the quality of the piece and your grade. The exercises in this section will allow you to practise your skills by looking carefully at how you structure your sentences, how you begin and end a piece of writing and the language and vocabulary that you choose.

Sentences

A. The length of sentences

In almost all forms of writing you can improve your style if you vary the length of your sentences. You should try to interweave longer, complex or compound sentences with shorter simple ones.

> She prepares a meal of tuna fish and salad and when they have eaten this food she makes the tea. They drink it, then wash the dishes up in an enamel basin. Miss Callgary disposes of the dregs from the teapot, and the tealeaves, in a small lavatory on a half landing, pouring away the washing-up water here also. No sound comes from the rooms below.
>
> **From *Felicia's Journey* by William Trevor (1994)**

Simple sentences contain just one clause. **Compound sentences** consist of two or more main clauses loosely joined by conjunctions – *and, or, but*. In **complex sentences**, clauses are linked together in ways which show the interrelationships between ideas. This involves the more sophisticated use of conjunctions or other linking devices.

If you begin a three-sentence paragraph with a longish sentence, then use a shorter one and end with a very short one it will almost certainly heighten the dramatic (or humorous) effect of your writing.

For example:

> After a while the old miller went away, leaving us at the mercy of the lice. He returned with a platter, a small bowl and three pairs of chopsticks, all of which he put on the quilt next to the lamp. Then he clambered onto the bed again.
>
> **From *Balzac and the Little Chinese Seamstress* by Dai Sijie (2000)**

> Stories handed down for hundreds of years are disappearing from our national consciousness. Far too many children now do not know European folk tales, Greek and Roman myths, Bible stories, Norse legends, Aesop's fables, the Arabian nights, Arthurian legends and so on. I find this worrying.
>
> **Susan Elkin, *Daily Telegraph* (25 May 1994)**

Or do it the other way round by starting with a short punchy sentence and becoming more expansive as the paragraph develops:

> I stopped and crunched the car into reverse. After a couple of hundred metres we had gathered speed and the Mazda's differential started to protest. Bob asked casually, almost gently so as not to distract my reverse driving concentration, 'Ever heard of a U-turn?'
>
> **From *Riding the Black Cockatoo* by John Danalis (2009)**

> Dave Pinchon was also arriving in an unfamiliar town. After having been in the column of schoolboys on the way to central station in Southampton, his next memory was of sitting with Bobby Mills on top of a rapidly emptying yellow double-decker bus as they went round Bournemouth. Eventually the bus arrived at a house that would take the two children and they disembarked.
>
> **From *Churchill's Children* by John Welshman (2010)**

Exercise 11

Below are two paragraphs using sentences of similar length, which makes them rather bland and boring. Rewrite the paragraphs (keeping the meaning the same) using sentences of varied length. Do not be afraid to ask a rhetorical question if you think it works in your writing.

a) The Briggs family visited Scotland last summer to find some traditional Highland clothing. In a shop in Inverness they found some excellent tartan fabric. But they couldn't find anyone selling the hand-knitted Shetland garments they wanted. They were disappointed when they had to leave Inverness empty handed.

b) In July 2005 it was announced that London had won the bid to host the 2012 Olympic Games. Most people regarded this as very good news and many media writers and speakers wrote and spoke very positively about it. The next day terrorist bombs on three underground trains and a bus killed 52 and injured 700 people who had been innocently travelling around the capital. No one has ever been quite sure whether or not there is, or was, a connection between these two happenings.

B. The shape of sentences

Do not get into the habit of beginning every sentence with the subject – a name, other form of noun, definite or indefinite articles ('a', 'an' or 'the') or a pronoun (such as 'it', 'this', 'he' or 'I').

Look at this example:

Version 1

Peter and Felix went to the skateboard park on Saturday. They like to go there almost every weekend. The skateboard park is near Felix's aunt's house. She often gives them tea and cake if they call in.

Version 2

Partly because it is near his aunt's house, Felix likes to go to the skateboard park with Peter most Saturdays as they did last weekend. They get tea and cake afterwards too.

Which is better?

Version 2 has more rhythm, flows better and is much less boring because the sentences have different shapes and lengths. Version 1 consists of four sentences each beginning with the subject of the sentence.

Techniques for varying sentence shape include the following four examples:

1. Starting with a fronted phrase or clause which usually qualifies, modifies or tells you more about the subject:

- Tired and dispirited, Mr Ericson …
- Always game for a joke, Peta …
- Wondering where the idea had come from, I …
- A black canvas with millions of diamond-like sparkles, the sky …

Note that such phrases and clauses are followed by a comma.

2. Beginning the sentence with an adverb:

- Angrily, he …
- Suddenly, Miss Rees …
- Later, we …

3. Using a sentence opener such as 'however', 'moreover' or 'therefore', which connects in some way to what has gone before:

- We have all read *As You Like It*. Moreover some of us went in a group to see it at Stratford.
- I love anything yellow. Therefore my bedroom is decorated in the sunniest shades I could find.

   (See other ways of using connectives on the following page.)

4. Writing reverse sentences in which what might have been the end of the sentence is put at the front with a conjunction in front of it:

- Because I didn't want to be late, I caught an earlier bus.
   (Instead of the more obvious 'I caught an earlier bus because I didn't want to be late.')
- While the teacher was talking, I made notes.
   (Instead of 'I made notes while the teacher was talking.')
- Although I don't usually like rice, I enjoy it when it's cooked Indian style.
   (Instead of 'I always eat it when it's cooked Indian style although I don't usually like rice.')

Look at the following sentence and then the many different ways of expressing more or less the same idea.

The biggest coincidence that day happened when Ella and I ended up sitting next to each other at Wembley Stadium.

- Coincidentally, Ella and I ended up sitting right next to each other at Wembley Stadium.
- What were the chances of my ending up sitting next to Ella at Wembley Stadium?
- When I sat down at Wembley Stadium, I realised that, by sheer coincidence I was sitting next to Ella.
- Sitting next to Ella at Wembley Stadium was a tremendous coincidence.
- Ella and I, without any prior planning, found ourselves sitting side by side at Wembley Stadium.
- Unbelievable I know, but Ella and I ended up sitting next to each other at Wembley Stadium.
- Many amazing coincidences occurred that day, but nothing topped sitting next to Ella at Wembley Stadium.
- By an extraordinary coincidence, Ella and I were seated side by side at Wembley Stadium.

Can you think of other variations?

Study
TIP

Find other examples of sentences and see how many different ways there are to express the same idea.

Exercise 12

Write as many variations as you can which mean roughly the same as these sentences:

a) My mother and father were both born in London but I was born in Somerset.

b) The dog stiffened and growled which was his way of telling us that something was seriously wrong.

c) One of my earliest memories is of blowing out the candles on my third birthday cake in my grandparents' house.

d) You must use good quality sieved flour and keep all the ingredients cool if you want to make really good pastry.

C. Using connectives

Connectives are words used within sentences to link parts together or to link one sentence with another.

Connectives can be conjunctions, adverbs, short phrases and other things. Good writing uses them a great deal.

To **add something** use: • and, also, as well as, moreover, too, furthermore, in addition.	To **qualify a statement** use: • however, although, unless, except, apart from, despite, in spite of.
To write about **cause and effect** use: • because, so, therefore, thus, consequently, as a result of.	To **be emphatic** use: • above all, in particular, especially, significantly, indeed, notably, most of all.
To **express ideas in sequence** or order use: • next, then, first, second, third, finally, meanwhile, after.	To **introduce an example** use: • for example, such as, for instance, as revealed by, in the case of, as shown by.
To **contrast something** with something else use: • whereas, instead of, alternatively, otherwise, unlike, on the other hand, in contrast.	To **compare one thing to another** use: • equally, in the same way, similarly, likewise, as with, compared with.

Examiner's TIP

Remember to vary the connectives you use in order to help make your writing more lively and interesting.

Beginnings and endings

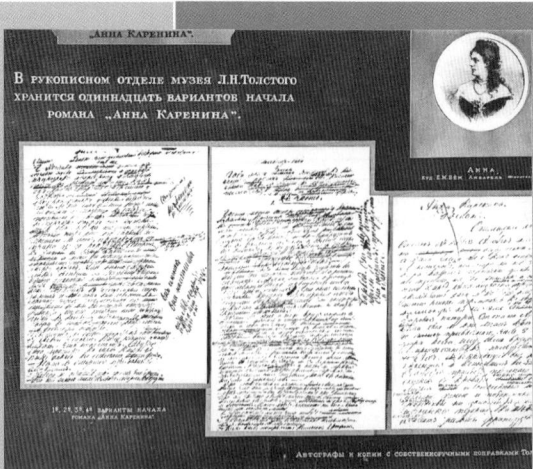

How do you start a story? You have an idea but somehow you have to break into it. For fairy or folk tales or pastiches of them we use the formulaic 'Once upon a time' but for most sorts of story this will not do. You have to find other ways of grabbing your reader's attention.

Here are some possibilities:

- Open with a snatch of conversation and then make it clear in the paragraph or so that follows what the situation is.
  'Let's put the tent here' said Jack, pointing to a patch of grass from which we could see the towering mountain we were aiming for . . .'

- Write something cryptic and confident to puzzle the reader so that he or she wants to read on to find out what the opening sentence means.
  'I've never liked ferrets ...' or 'Henry Betts's head was bald ...'.

- Make a statement that will relate to your story.
  'If you scratch a sore spot it will get sorer. And the same applies to friendship ...'

Read the examples opposite of how to start a piece of writing.

'I have been in love with Titus Oates for quite a while now – which is ridiculous since he's been dead for ninety years.' **From *The White Darkness* by Geraldine McCaughrean (2005)**
'Last night I dreamt I went to Manderley again.' **From *Rebecca* by Daphne Du Maurier (1938)**
'All happy families are alike but an unhappy family is unhappy after its own fashion.' **From *Anna Karenina* by Leo Tolstoy (1878)**
'Aujourd'hui Maman est morte.' (Mother died today.) **From *L'Etranger* by Albert Camus (1942)**
'When in Rome (said Sandor) you have to walk down the Via Condotti and look at the shops.' **From *Gallowglass* by Barbara Vine (1990)**
'Things started to fall apart at home when my brother Jaja did not go to communion and Papa flung his heavy missal across the room and broke the figurines on the étagère.' **From *Purple Hibiscus* by Chimamanda Ngozi Adichie (2004)**
'The men in the office all went bananas when Bambi arrived.' **From 'The Bimbo' short story in *Bread and Chocolate* by Philippa Gregory (2000)**
'It is a truth universally acknowledged, that a single man in possession of a good fortune, must be in want of a wife,' **From *Pride and Prejudice* by Jane Austen (1813)**
'In the beginning God created the heaven and the earth.' **From 'Genesis' in the Authorised Version of *The Bible* (translated 1611)**

Study TIP

When you are reading fiction look carefully at the story or novel's opening sentence. What has the author done to make you read on? You may be able to use techniques you spot while reading in your own writing.

A. Different approaches

Non-fiction writing sometimes uses a different approach to beginnings and endings. Newspaper or magazine articles that express an opinion or argue a point of view typically open with an anecdote (little story) or personal statement, move away from it in the main body of the writing and refer back to it at the end. Think of it like this:

- opening
- points to be made, argument to be developed or other evidence
- conclusion, making some reference to the opening.

So, if you were writing about maths teaching you might start:	My mother always told me I couldn't do maths. Perhaps she thinks that because she couldn't and neither can any of the other women in my family.
You could continue:	But in my case she was wrong … (points about the fine maths teachers who have worked with you, modern 'can do' approach, effects of technology, changing opportunities for mathematicians, why you like it or excel at it, etc.).
You could end:	So, all in all, maths and me are a pretty good match and thank goodness I've gone through school at a time which has made it possible. And, as for my mother, I'm not sure whether she is pleased or sorry that I've broken the family mould.

Study TIP Read as many opinion and comment columns as you can in newspapers, magazines or on the internet. Look carefully at how they are structured so that you can use similar techniques in your own writing.

Vocabulary

The more words you know and can use, the better your writing will be because you will be able to choose the exact vocabulary you need – as if you had a thesaurus programmed into the hard drive of your brain!

English has an immense lexicon (bank of words). There are at least 500,000 words in everyday use in English compared with around 200,000 in French and 150,000 in German.

That is why there are so many fine shades of meaning in English words. Consider, for example, the differences between the words in each of these lists:

- necklace, locket, pendant, chain, beads, necklet, choker
- kill, murder, assassinate, execute, butcher, slaughter, exterminate
- observant, watchful, attentive, vigilant
- politely, civilly, courteously, respectfully, graciously
- teacher, tutor, educator, instructor, trainer, mentor.

It is very rare for two words in English to be exact synonyms – identical in meaning. Each of the words in the lists above has a precise meaning which differentiates it from the other words in its group, although each group also has a certain amount of meaning in common.

A. Using vocabularly accurately

Good writers choose the word that means exactly what they want to say. Accurate vocabulary choices tend to make writing more concise because words are not wasted.

If you are writing about the wooden border at the base of the wall into which an electric socket is often mounted, it is much more incisive if you refer to it accurately as a skirting board.

It is usually better to write 'She lolloped across the field' than 'She ran across the field in a slow, plodding, clumsy way as if she couldn't quite control her legs and arms'.

But – and it is quite a big but – beware of two things:

1. Do not use a long word where a short one will do, simply because you know the longer word and think it sounds more impressive. Do not write 'peregrinate' if you actually mean walk, 'veracity' if you mean truth or 'iracund' when you mean cross, unless you are trying to create some sort of special effect such as making a character sound verbose or pompous.

2. Do not clutter your work with extra adjectives and adverbs (as you may have been advised to do when you were younger) in an attempt to make it sound interesting. Instead, choose strong accurate nouns and verbs wherever you can.

For example, use:

- **tyrant** instead of dictatorial and utterly ruthless man
- **strode** instead of walked determinedly
- **gobbled** instead of ate hungrily
- **capital** rather than all the money, saved, accumulated or borrowed, that she had in the bank with which to start her business.

Study TIP

How do you acquire an extensive vocabulary?

It comes, of course, as teachers have been telling you for as long as you can remember, from **reading** – widely and continually.

By reading every day you will absorb vocabulary and learn how to express yourself in different ways and in different styles.

You should read:

- fiction books (short stories are good if you are too busy to get involved with a novel)
- non-fiction books or parts of them
- newspapers (just read what interests you – there is no law that says you have to read every word – and you can read many newspapers online if you prefer)
- magazines
- internet sites with articles, reviews, etc.

Reading isn't a luxury or an extra; it is essential.

'Appropriate' language

OCR examiners say that they will award higher marks to candidates who:

- make choices in their writing that are appropriate to audience and purpose
- make sure spelling, punctuation and grammatical structures are accurate and appropriate for purpose and effect.

These two 'descriptors' (as examiners call them) apply to all GCSE examining boards and to IGCSE.

'Appropriate to audience and purpose' means that you can break away from conventional grammar rules and other habits of 'good English' if you are writing for a purpose that requires you to do so.

For example, if you were writing dialogue between two teenage boys in a dark block of flats in an inner city area who rarely attend school and are planning a robbery, you would probably make their language more colloquial and less 'correct' than if your characters were two retired teachers chatting on a seaside bench in Bournemouth – or if you were using your own voice to express an opinion in a non-fiction piece.

If you are writing a fictional first-person piece, your character may have a distinctive 'voice' that means he or she uses language sloppily, wordily, self-importantly, nervously – or in some other way depending on the effect that you are trying to create. Sue Townsend's Adrian Mole books are a good example of this.

> **Study TIP**
>
> Look at these two books to see how the professionals use appropriate language for their purpose:
>
> In *Cat's Eye* by Margaret Atwood (1988), the narrator, Elaine Risley, uses the run-on comma (much loathed by English teachers normally) throughout the novel to suggest her breathy, ill-at-ease personality.
>
> *Flowers for Algernon* by Daniel Keyes (1969) is a science fiction story told as a series of progress reports by mentally disabled Charlie who has undergone controversial surgery. At first his English is very limited. As his condition improves the language becomes very accurate and fluent before declining again at the end.

Section Five

GCSE and IGCSE English (as opposed to English Literature) examinations always include some work on written texts. Literature is, of course, part of all English studies.

But be careful about the term English Literature, because so many of the texts we study in school are American (*To Kill a Mockingbird*, *Of Mice and Men*), Australian (*Riding the Black Cockatoo*), African (*Purple Hibiscus*) and so on. Some people use the term 'Literature in English', which seems to cover all texts.

Many of you will be taking GCSE or IGCSE English Literature alongside GCSE or IGCSE English – taught by the same teacher in the same lessons. Obviously, for your English Literature papers and assessments, all the tasks will relate to texts you have studied or are given to read in the examination, but, as mentioned in Section 2, for GCSE and IGCSE English you will also have to write about texts, some of them literary.

> **Study TIP**
>
> There is no substitute for reading and re-reading your set texts so that you know them as well as you possibly can. Aim to have read each text at least three times before the examination. During the revision period divide each set text into manageable chunks – perhaps a chapter, scene or poem per day for the two months preceding the examination.

A literature-related task at GCSE or IGCSE usually takes one of the following forms:

- Examine and analyse a short piece of text – poetry or prose – a copy of which you have in front of you. It may be part of something you have studied in advance or it may be new to you.
- Compare two short pieces – usually poems.
- Comment on a longer work of literature such as a novel or play, which you have worked on in depth and at length in class. The task usually asks you to write about plot, character or theme or a combination of these, but to achieve A* you should also think about the subtext of the question – what is the writing doing, how is he/she doing it and why. Whether or not you have the text with you to refer to depends on the rules set by your examination board for this part of your assessment.
- Write about a novel or a play by imagining that you are one of the characters – this is often known as an empathy question because you are being asked to empathise with someone.

> **Study TIP**
>
> Many candidates find that they know the beginning of a novel or play much better than the end – perhaps because they have read the opening several times but not always read through to the end. Get round this by starting in the middle and reading to the end as part of your revision. After all, you know the work well enough by now to know what is going on in the plot. Another revision strategy, which works for some people, is to read the work backwards once – start with the last chapter or section and read the rest in reverse order.

Detailed analysis of a short piece

Practise the skills required for analysing a short piece by:

- Selecting short sections of the novel or play you have studied, setting yourself tasks on it and practising writing them in 40 minutes or so. Bear in mind that examiners often ask you to relate the extract to the rest of the book or play too.
- Looking through a poetry anthology such as *The Dragon Book of Verse*, *Touched with Fire* or *Poets of Our Time* (all of which will probably be in the English Department at your school, full details below), selecting poems of 20 to 30 lines and asking yourself what you could write about each poem if you were presented with it in an examination.

The New Dragon Book of Verse, ed Michael Harrison & Christopher Stuart-Clark, OUP, 1989, ISBN 9780198312413

Touched with Fire, ed Jack Hydes, CUP, 1985, ISBN 9780521315371

Poets of Our Time, ed F E S Finn, John Murray, 1965, ISBN 9780719504402

Technical devices

When you are writing about poetry (and, to an extent, prose too) you will be expected to notice and comment on how the writer achieves his or her effects.

Read through this list of nine technical terms and think about the effect that each device creates:

Alliteration – the repetition of the same letter at the beginning of neighbouring words. You can also use the adjective 'alliterative'.	'Slowly, silently now the moon. Walks the night in her silver shoon' **From 'Silver' by Walter de la Mare** 'But day doth daily draw my sorrows longer' **From 'Sonnet 28' by William Shakespeare**
Assonance – the repetition of the same vowel sound (not necessarily spelt the same way) inside neighbouring words. You can also use the adjective 'assonant'.	'Meekly kneeling upon your knees' **From the Book of Common Prayer** 'A snake came to my water trough' **From 'Snake' by D H Lawrence** 'Willows whiten, aspens quiver, Little breezes dusk and shiver' **From 'The Lady of Shallott' by Alfred Lord Tennyson**
Caesura – a break in a line of poetry. This was usual in Latin poetry and still exists in some English poetry. The caesura in the below examples is illustrated with a /. You will notice that caesura is sometimes made more obvious through the use of punctuation, while at other times there is no punctuation present.	'Being your slave, / what should I do but tend' **From 'Sonnet 57' by William Shakespeare** 'I fondly ask: / But patience to prevent' **From 'On his Blindness' by John Milton** 'The Assyrians came down / like a wolf on the fold. And his cohorts were gleaming / in purple and gold.' **From 'The Destruction of Sennacherib' by Lord Byron**

Consonance – the repetition of consonant sounds (not necessarily spelt the same) inside neighbouring words. In this example the repeated 'm' sounds create a hum like the plaintive wail of bagpipes. You can also use the adjective 'consonant' in a sentence such as: 'The consonant "m" underpinning these three lines gives them a mournful, soulful atmosphere.'	'Age shall not weary the**m**, nor the years conde**m**n. At the going down of the sun and in the **m**orning We will re**mem**ber the**m**' **From 'For the Fallen' by Laurence Binyon**
Enjambement – the continuation of meaning from one line or verse of poetry into the next so that the sentence (as it were) does not end at the end of the line or verse.	'When fishes flew and forests walked And figs grew upon thorn, Some moment when the moon was blood Then surely I was born.' **From 'The Donkey' by G K Chesterton** 'As a child at dream, at a jaguar hurrying enraged Through prison darkness after the drills of his eyes On a short fierce fuse ...' **From 'The Jaguar' by Ted Hughes**
Metaphor – the comparison of one thing with another by pretending that the thing described really is what it is being compared with. Like personification or a simile (see below), a metaphor is a form of image. The adjective 'metaphorical' and the adverb 'metaphorically' are useful too. Metaphors are not *literally* true.	'And their great hulks were seraphim of gold, Or mute ecstatic monsters on the mould.' **From 'Horses' by Edwin Muir** 'Some goldfish in a bowl quietly sculled Around their shining prison on its shelf' **From 'The Lesson' by Edward Lucie Smith**
Onomatopoeia – the use of words to imitate sounds. A single word, like 'sizzle', can be onomatopoeic, but poets also often put words together onomatopoeically. In this example the repeated hissing or sibilant and z sounds suggest the sound of the insects.	'... hushed with buzzing night flies ...' **From *Henry IV Part 2* by William Shakespeare**
Personification – the giving of human qualities and abilities to non-humans. Poets often personify things as a way of describing them. It creates an image or picture in the reader's mind.	'Her brothers were the craggy hills Her sisters larchen trees' **From 'Meg Merrilees' by John Keats** 'Spring, the sweet Spring, is the year's pleasant king' **From 'Spring' by Thomas Nashe** '... the wheel's kick and the wind's song ...' **From 'Sea Fever' by John Masefield**
Simile – a comparison of one thing with another which makes it clear that it is a comparison by using the word 'like' or 'as'. It is yet another sort of image.	'Pity, like a naked new born babe' **From *Macbeth* by William Shakespeare** 'As traceless as a thaw of bygone snow' **From 'Sonnet' by Christina Rossetti**

None of these devices work in a self-contained way. Writers – especially poets – use them in stunning combinations to achieve their effects. Many of the examples above could be used to illustrate several devices.

Examiner's TIP

The examiner will not give any marks for 'device spotting'. It is not enough to write that the poet or author has used, say, a metaphor. You are expected to comment on the **effect** of the metaphor.

One trick to make sure that you go beyond device spotting is to use the adjectival form of the word rather than the noun. If you write 'The alliterative/metaphorical/ onomatopoeic effect is ...' it forces you to make a statement about it.

For example:

> I wandered lonely as a cloud
> That floats on high o'er vales and hills
> When all at once I saw a crowd
> A host of golden daffodils;
> Beside the lake, beneath the trees,
> Fluttering and dancing in the breeze.
>
> **William Wordsworth, 1770–1850**

First the narrator compares himself with a single cloud as he wanders alone 'o'er hills and vales' and this simile creates a sense of a solitary, serious and rather remote observer who is suddenly struck with earthy joy when he sees the daffodils. The imagery he uses to describe the daffodils marks a sudden turning point in the poem – like an unexpected loud climax in music. The 'fluttering and dancing' daffodils are full of movement and Wordsworth personifies them as a crowd (which would be people) or a host (the collective noun for angels which befits their 'golden' colour) because there are so many of them – in contrast to the 'lonely' narrator. The assonance in 'host of golden daffodils' and the rhythm it helps to create makes the second three lines move faster and more joyfully than the first three, which are largely monosyllabic.

Exercise 13

Read this extract from 'Composed Upon Westminster Bridge, September 3, 1802' by William Wordsworth and identify the use of simile, alliteration, personification and assonance.

Make notes on how Wordsworth has used these techniques and the effects of each technique.

The City now doth, like a garment, wear
The beauty of the morning; silent, bare,
Ships, towers, domes, theatres and temples lie
Open unto the fields and to the sky

Appropriate language

You need a good bank of appropriate vocabulary for writing detailed comments on works of literature. You could start your sentences with:

The author/writer/poet/playwright:

- suggests
- implies
- hints
- creates
- wonders
- asks
- argues
- states
- asserts
- depicts
- insists
- conveys
- questions ...

Examiner's TIP

- English literature does not have right and wrong answers.
- No two answers, even if they score the same marks, will make exactly the same points.
- You can answer a question in more than one way and still score high marks.

Remember that it is rare for two words in English to have identical meanings. Each of these verbs has a precise meaning of its own and so they are not interchangeable.

Other useful expressions include:

The author/writer/poet/playwright:

- focuses on
- draws attention to
- wonders whether
- asks us
- reflects on
- creates a situation in which ...

Examiner's TIP

Refer to the writer by his or her surname or forename and surname, for example:
- Shakespeare, Charles Dickens, Christina Rossetti, Orwell, Lee, Steinbeck, Duffy
Never use just the writer's forename: William, Christina, Charles, George, Harper, John, Carol!

Try to use the author's name (or refer to him or her) at least once in every paragraph. It helps to ensure that you are writing critically and not just retelling the story. Make statements such as:

- Harper Lee makes us aware ...
- The poet presents ...
- The author makes it clear that ...
- Shakespeare evidently sympathises with ...
- Doyle makes Paddy say ... (in reference to *Paddy Clarke Ha Ha Ha* by Roddy Doyle)
- Dickens tells us through Pip ...
- Wilfred Owen wants the reader to know that ...

Comparisons

If you are asked to compare and/or contrast Text A with Text B, there are three ways of doing it:

1. Write about A. Write about B. Then comment on differences and similarities.

2. Write about A and then present B in comparison to what is written about A.

3. Write about one aspect of A comparing and/or contrasting it with B as you go along. Then move on to another aspect. Aim to cover four or five aspects in your answer.

The second and especially the third of these will produce much better answers and are the methods used by almost all candidates achieving A and A* grades.

If you use the first method you run the risk of barely making any comparison at all because it has to be squeezed, like an afterthought, into the last third of your answer.

The second method does risk your writing more about A than B, resulting in an uneven answer.

Examiner's TIP

When you are making comparisons and commenting on differences and similarities between the texts, use expressions such as:

- On the other hand ...
- Unlike Text A, Text B ...
- In a similar way, Text A ...
- But the writer of Text B takes a different approach ...
- Similarly, Text B ...
- In contrast, Text A ...
- Text B is quite different. It ...
- In another mood is Text B, which ...

Be sure to use the surnames of the writers of the texts you are comparing.

Essays on studied works of literature

The types of question you are likely to be asked at GCSE and IGCSE are based on character and theme. In order to answer these questions effectively you must have a thorough knowledge of the plot:

Plot – what happens in the novel/play and how the author makes it interesting.

Characters – who is in the novel/play and how they develop.

Themes – what are the main ideas and messages running through the novel/play.

The works referred to in this section are *To Kill a Mockingbird* by Harper Lee and *Macbeth* by William Shakespeare.

Planning

Always work out what the question is asking you to do and make a plan before you begin. In an exam, when you are under time pressure, you will have to do this very quickly. First, use a highlighter to emphasise the key words in the question. Or underline them.

Second, devise an essay plan. Even 2–5 minutes spent on making a plan will pay off. Your answer will be better thought out and shaped and you are less likely to miss out important points if you've noted them first in your plan. This could be the difference between getting a lower grade and an A*.

Experiment with different sorts of plan and decide what works for you. Some people like diagrammatic plans. That usually means putting the key idea in a circle at the centre of the page. The main points to be included in the essay then go in other circles elsewhere on the paper linked to it. Alternatively just number the points. This is how a quick sketch plan might look for the question *Atticus tells Scout that you don't really know a man 'until you stand in his shoes and walk around in them.' What does Lee show us that Scout has learned about life from other people's perspectives by the end of the novel?*

Examiner's TIP

You will know the text very well indeed by the time you take your exam and could not possibly write down everything that you know about it. So don't try to! The skill is to select from the large amount that you know the – relatively few – points that you will need for your examination answer. That is why planning is so important.

Examiner's TIP

Try to plan your time carefully so that you always complete your answer. If, however, you misjudge the time and don't finish, hand in your plan so that the examiner can see where your answer was going.

1. Introduction: A makes comment about BR. Also applies - Bob E, Mrs D, Aunt A.

2. BR presented as Scout's main lesson – from tormenting in ch 1 etc to complete understanding at end. (Radley porch = symbol)

3. Bob E vicious & lazy – Scout knows no one else like this. Understands eventually he's better dead. Sympathy for Mayella though – trial etc.

4. Mrs D seems spiteful (Lee's presentation) – until Scout learns otherwise

5. Aunt A friction with S, at first. Gradual dev't of respect for her point of view – she's right about Bob E.

6. Conclusion: TKaMB could be subtitled 'What Scout Learns.' HL details S's mental dev't age 6-9 and uses incidents to shape it.

Always 'frame' your answer with an introduction and a conclusion. You are unlikely to be able to make more than four or five main points in the body of your answer in the time available to you in a GCSE or IGCSE exam.

Essay openings

You will get no marks for writing out the question in your opening sentence or paragraph. Instead your introduction might:

- say how you're going to tackle the question
- interpret the question – say what you think it means
- comment on something in the question
- make some general introductory remarks.

Essay endings

You will get no extra marks for merely repeating in your conclusion something that you've already said. In your conclusion you might:

- summarise your arguments and draw them together in a new way
- make a new point which you have deliberately held back for the ending
- try to be 'punchy' so that there is a sense of an essay which has been finished rather than just allowed to tail off.

Examiner's TIP

Always plan your time in the examination carefully. Divide your time between tasks so that you give each one proper attention. If there are, say, two tasks with the marks divided equally between them you cannot get more than 50 per cent for the first so do not spend more than half your time on it.

Examiner's TIP

Imagine the examiner reading your answer with his or her red pen in hand. Give the examiner something to tick and it will score marks. You score marks for making informed analytical comment. Don't waste your (very limited) time writing anything else.

Examiner's TIP

The examiner is interested in *your* response to the books you have studied and what you think about them.

Using evidence in essays

Just as scientists must provide evidence to back up their theories so you, as the writer of an English Literature essay, need evidence to back up yours.

Unlike a scientist, however, you don't need to look far for it. All the evidence you need is in the text you are writing about.

There are two sorts of evidence:

1. quotation of exact words. Look for short phrases in the text that illustrate your points and then weave them into your sentences. Always remember to put inverted commas ('quotation marks') around them.

You will never need to quote more than one sentence at a time. Aim to work at least eight direct quotations into an examination essay.

Structure your sentences like these examples, which relate to *To Kill a Mockingbird*:

Once Jem is twelve, Scout finds him 'inconsistent' and 'moody', but Calpurnia, ever perceptive, tells her 'not to fret too much' because the maturing Jem will need to be 'off to himself' and 'doing whatever boys do'.

As Harper Lee builds up the tension, Scout suddenly realises that their 'company' in the wood has 'shuffled and dragged his feet' before she hears 'running towards us with no child's feet'.

2. reference to incidents. These references do not require direct quotations.

In *Macbeth*, for example, you might refer in general terms to the waiting woman's conversation with the doctor about Lady Macbeth's sleepwalking, Malcolm's long stay in England or Macbeth's reaction to the messenger's news about the approaching soldiers.

Study TIP

As you re-read and revise your set texts, copy short important quotations (ideally half a sentence or less) into a small notebook. Carry this everywhere with you in your bag or pocket. Look at it and keep revising these quotations at odd moments such as at the bus stop, in a queue or while you are waiting for someone or something. The 'drip feed' method is a very effective way of learning for many people.

Examiner's TIP

Refer to things that happen in the text you are writing about as:

• incidents
• scenes
• happenings
• occasions
• events
• episodes.

Exercise 14

These examples all relate to *To Kill a Mockingbird* by Harper Lee and *Macbeth* by William Shakespeare, both popular GCSE texts. Substitute similar questions, modelled on these, relating to 'your' novel and play if you are not studying *To Kill a Mockingbird* or *Macbeth*. Remember to consider the writer's perspective and the subtext of the question.

These questions focus on the **plot**:

a) Atticus tells Scout that you don't really know a man 'until you stand in his shoes and walk around in them'. What does Lee show us that Scout has learned about life from other people's perspectives by the end of the novel?

b) How important are the witches in *Macbeth*?

These questions ask you to think about **characters** and how the author presents them:

c) How do the characters of Jem and Scout change and grow up during the novel?

d) How does the character of Macbeth change during the play?

These questions ask you to unravel and analyse a major **theme** in the text:

e) How is the theme of racial prejudice presented in *To Kill a Mockingbird*?

f) How does Shakespeare present the theme of power in *Macbeth*?

Study TIP Devise writing assignments similar to the ones you will be set in your examination papers (your teachers will have told you what to expect). Swap them with a friend and practise writing answers to time.

Ten don'ts for literature-related essay writing

(1) *Don't* retell the story.

(2) *Don't* make vague statements for which you have no evidence.

(3) *Don't* waste your time writing out long quotations that aren't grafted tightly into your arguments.

(4) *Don't* begin sentences or paragraphs 'The above quotation shows …'.

(5) *Don't* use slang or colloquialisms.

(6) *Don't* try to write everything you know about the text.

(7) *Don't* misspell the names of characters and places in the text, or the name of the author.

(8) *Don't* confuse the author with his or her fictional, first-person narrator.

(9) *Don't* overlook the importance of writing within the time available.

(10) *Don't* forget to leave yourself a few minutes at the end to check your spelling and punctuation.

Empathy essays

Some examination boards sometimes give students the opportunity to show knowledge and understanding of texts they have studied by imagining themselves into the 'skin' of one of the characters.

This is an interesting approach and it's a good creative challenge. Some students think it is easier because it doesn't call for the use of technical literary vocabulary or formal language. In fact, it is just as demanding as writing a traditional English Literature essay. You still have to show detailed knowledge and understanding of the text and its plot, characters and themes. You must not invent details of your own and everything you write must be rooted firmly in the pages of the text. You also need some sense of the voice of the character you are empathising with and how he or she would speak or write.

The example which follows relates to the novel *Anita and Me* by Meera Syal, another widely set GCSE text. Meena Kumar is the narrator of the novel. Even if you are not studying this text and/or have not read it, this essay – which was graded A* – should give you some idea of what you're aiming for if you choose, or are given the opportunity, to write a GCSE or IGCSE empathy essay.

The empathy essay on the following pages is annotated to indicate the methods that can be used to improve your own writing as identified in Section 4 (see pages 32–43).

achieve grade A

Imagine you are Meena's father. At the end of the novel you think back over your life so far. Write down your thoughts and feelings.

Strong opening statement

Partition and its horrors led directly to my living for thirteen years in Tollington near Wolverhampton with my beloved, petite, beautifully mannered wife Daljit. Both our children were born while we were there: Meena a year or two after we arrived and Sunil a decade later.

I was born in 1930 **and** grew up in Lahore but when India was split and Pakistan created **after** my country gained independence from the British there was terrible suffering and violence. My family was one of millions living on the 'wrong' side of the border. **That is why** I spent my 17th birthday in a refugee camp. I ended up in Delhi **where** I went to university (**although** my arts degree wasn't to prove very useful when I ended up in accountancy in Britain). I met and married my lovely Daljit in Dehli **where** she was training to be a teacher. We worked there **for a while but then** decided that India had become no place for people **who** were both poor and clever and that opportunities for our children would be better in Britain.

Useful connective words and phrases in bold

I came on my own to find a job and somewhere to live before Daljit joined me. How well I remember arriving in London with just £25 in my pocket. Amman spotted me at Paddington and befriended me and we often laugh about that at our musical evenings. We had such a lot in common. He and Shaila have been our dearest friends ever since. They lived just a few miles from us while we were in Tollington and then, when Meena started at the Grammar School we moved into a four-bedroomed bungalow near them.

Sentence shape varies

So why Tollington? It was a former mining village in a depressed area so we were able to buy a two bedroomed house very cheaply. It was a pretty basic miner's cottage without bathroom and only an outside privy opening onto a communal yard at the back but it was a start and we could afford it. Daljit, who taught infants at the village school, liked it too because the open fields opposite reminded her of the wide spaces of India and she was often deeply homesick for the people and places we had left behind – especially our four aging parents.

Accurate vocabulary

Of course we weren't that happy about Meena's friendship with Miss Anita Rutter which began when our daughter was about nine. She picked up some bad ways. I never really believed, for example, that it was Shaila and Amman's delightfully demure girls, Pinky and Baby, who stole that collection tin from Mr Ormerod's shop when Meena took them there with Anita. And who on earth had Meena picked up that outrageously coarse slang 'shagged the arse' from? It must have been Anita. It must also have been Anita who talked to her about being a virgin – which did not please me at all. Well behaved Indian girls simply should not be thinking about such things.

Accurate vocabulary

On the other hand Meena had to live and go to school in Tollington and we felt it was right that she should be part of the community. We knew (hoped fervently!) that she would pass her exam and get to the grammar school when she was eleven at which point she would leave Anita and the other village children behind and make new friends. Although Daljit was furious with the Rutters for calling their dog 'Nigger,' she felt desperately sorry for Anita when her mother walked out which is why we invited her for a meal – not a resounding success, as it turned out.

Appropriate tone, register and style for Mr Kumar

I was always quite happy, moreover, when Meena was at the church – I have **rejected** religion for myself having seen the damage it can do but believe in being **tolerant** of other people's views – with that sensitive and educated Mr Alan who led a lot of community projects and kept the children usefully occupied.

Accurate vocabulary in bold

We had some challenging times in Tollington, though. Daljit found life very difficult after Sunil was born. He was a very demanding baby and I suppose Daljit's problem was a form of post-natal depression. I had to find a solution quickly so I managed to arrange for Daljit's mother to come to Britain for an extended stay. The visit was a huge success. My mother-in-law sorted out Sunil's feeding and sleeping routines and had a wonderful effect on Meena who learned Punjabi rapidly in order to understand her Nanima's stories. We were delighted to see our daughter really beginning to connect with her heritage. It put new life into Daljit too.

Sentence shape varies

Then there was Meena's accident. She fell from a horse at the farm with the other girls, although we never quite got to the bottom of how she came to be riding it so fast and apparently on her own. It put her in hospital from late August to Christmas and even then, when they took the cast off her leg it was alarmingly wasted. She seemed to grow up a lot while she was there partly because she became sweet on a boy named Robert who was dying, and actually died a few days after she was discharged. I think all of that made her think hard about what friendship really means. I'm sure she evaluated her relationship with Anita too.

Detailed reference to text

One of the worst nights of our lives was just a few months before we left Tollington. We had a call to tell us that Amman was having emergency surgery and Shaila was desperate for support at the hospital. So, reluctantly, we left Meena alone in the house. Although

Good use of detail

she hadn't had anything much to do with the Rutters for months she went out in the night with Tracey. Something was going on in the grounds of the big house. Anita and that Sam Lowbridge of course... Tracey fell in the lake and Meena had to run for help. When we got news of this we thought at first that it was Meena who'd had the accident. So it was a frightening business although young Tracey survived unscathed against all the odds.

Accurate spelling and punctuation

The good thing which came out of that was that the owner of The Big House turned out to be Indian! All the years we'd lived there and we had no idea, although he knew about us. I went to tea with him afterwards and he tipped me off that I should get the house on the market immediately because of building plans for Tollington which, by then, was changing rapidly.

I'm still only in my early forties. I've just had a promotion at work. Meena is about to start at the grammar school and we now live in a good area near our friends. Meena once described me as having 'a peculiar brand of fiery caution.' Perhaps she is right, but as she also says it is probably inevitable because, like everyone else in my generation and from my background, I have already taken enough risks to last a lifetime.

Quotation well used

Decisive conclusion

An extra challenge...

Here are two examples of empathy essay-type questions for you to practise with:

- **Imagine you are Macduff. Look back on your life and write about your feelings at the end of *Macbeth*.**

- **Pretend that you are George and write your statement for the police at the end of *Of Mice and Men* when you are arrested for murder. Include the circumstances of Lennie's life and death and your feelings about everything which has happened.**

Again, try substituting similar questions, modelled on these, relating to 'your' novel and play.

Accuracy Section

Achieving A* through accuracy

As well as reading carefully and writing perceptive and imaginative answers, you need to show GCSE or IGCSE examiners that you can write with precision and that you understand the nuts and bolts of the English language. This means paying close attention to grammar, punctuation and spelling.

Although you will not be asked specific questions about grammar or punctuation in your assessments, some of the marks at GCSE and IGCSE depend upon the use of accurate, appropriate language, including punctuation and spelling. Also, if you have good background knowledge of the structure of sentences, and the different sorts of words that go into a good sentence, you are more likely to write well.

'Students will demonstrate their ability to make sure that spelling, punctuation and grammatical structures are accurate and appropriate for purpose and effect.'
Edexcel GCSE English Language specification

'Candidates should be able to write accurately and fluently.'
OCR GCSE English specification

Grammar

Grammar is a huge subject. Sometimes it's tricky too because experts have a habit of disagreeing about the finer points. You will, long before you started your GCSE or IGCSE course, have worked on grammar in your English lessons. Obviously, this section cannot cover the whole of English grammar but what follows are the particularly important points that it is useful to remember.

If there are any other points of grammar that you are not sure about after you have worked through this section then ask a teacher for help.

'Appropriate' grammar

All GCSE and IGCSE examiners stress that candidates' use of language should be appropriate for its purpose rather than 'correct' or 'conventional'.

So, what do they mean by that? In formal English – the kind written by news reporters in newspapers or spoken by the Queen in her Christmas message to the nation – the language consists of carefully structured, full sentences and follows certain rules. This is what you should aim for in your assessments when you are expressing an opinion, writing some kind of report or commenting formally on a text you have read.

On the other hand, in everyday life, people continually break grammar rules, particularly in speech. Few people always use whole sentences all the time and some hardly ever use one. Small children tend not to use grammar conventionally ('Sophie and me buying it by ourselves') and there are many dialects in English in which people speak or write in different ways, for example:

"Yus you dessay! I know. Every loafer that can't do nothink calls hisself a painter. Well I'm a real painter: grainer, finisher, thirty-eight bob a week when I can get it."
From *Major Barbara* by George Bernard Shaw (1905)

In this competition
dey was looking for poetry of worth
for a writing that could wrap up a feelin
an fling it back hard
with a captive power to choke de stars
so dey say
'Send them to us
but NO DIALECTS PLEASE'
We're British!
From 'No Dialects Please' by Merle Collins (1987)

When you are writing you have to choose what sort of grammar to use according to what it is you are writing and the impression you want to create. If, for example, the character you are creating would break the rules, then you are free to do so.

In practice, it is very unlikely that you will be able to do this with confidence and flair (and so score high marks) unless you understand the conventions that you are deliberately breaking. For that reason, it is worth reminding yourself of the basics.

Word classes

Here, and on the following five pages, is a brief summary of the word classes (or parts of speech) and how they work.

Remember that words are not loyal. They belong to different groups depending on the job they are required to do in a particular sentence.

Nouns

A noun is a naming word. There are several sorts:

Study TIP
Common, proper and collective nouns are also known as concrete nouns. They are 'concrete' rather than abstract. 'Sophisticate', 'honey' and 'humorist' are concrete nouns; 'sophistication', 'mellifluousness' and 'hilarity' are abstract nouns.

- **common** – for example: pen, computer, shirt, girl
- **proper** – for example: Birmingham, Prince Harry, Starbucks, River Tweed
- **abstract** – for example: silence, laughter, desire, thoughtlessness
- **collective** – for example: pride (of lions), choir (of singers), host (of angels), set (of tools)

Verbs

A verb is an action or 'being' word, which shows you what is happening in a sentence.

Verbs can be expressed in various versions of the past, present and future tenses depending on when the action or situation took, takes or will take place.

In sentences, verbs often consist of two or more words because they sometimes use auxiliary (helping) verbs – 'to have' or 'to be' – to show the tense.

- We **chorused** all the songs we knew.
- Mr Ericson **is** the principal of our college.
- '**Run** faster!' **shouted** the Olympic coach.
- We **are** the champions.

- By September we **shall have been** students in this school for five years.
- Ella **was cycling** through the town centre.
- You **will be** late for your science practical.
- **Has** she **been reading** *The Da Vinci Code*?

Study TIP
When you are reading and commenting on texts look out for the difference between the simple and continuous tenses because they affect the tone of the writing. Think about the difference in effect of 'they strove' (simple past tense) and 'they were striving' (continuous past tense). In her 2004 novel *Purple Hibiscus*, Chimamanda Ngozi Adichie writes: 'Father Amadi's face was looking down at me when I opened my eyes' (continuous past tense). What difference would it have made if she had used the simple past tense and written 'looked'?

Adjectives

Adjectives are describing words, which 'qualify' or 'modify' – tell you more about – nouns.

- I prefer **cool, crisp winter** days to **dull, mild** ones.
- Drink your **hot** chocolate before it gets **cold**.
- **Blue** hyacinths are my **favourite** flowers.

They can be used in a comparative (more) form:

- sillier, more beautiful, worse.

Or a superlative (most) form:

- silliest, most beautiful, worst.

Adverbs

Adverbs are describing words, which 'qualify' or 'modify' – tell you more about – verbs. They usually tell you how, when, where or why something happens.

- Harry Potter and his friends ate **hungrily**.
- My car accelerates **rapidly**.
- We did it **yesterday**.
- Her cousins live **nearby**.

Adverbs also sometimes qualify other adverbs or adjectives.

- My brother was **unusually** quiet.
- **Surprisingly** light traffic meant that we got there **quite** quickly.
- 'To die would be an **awfully** big adventure,' is the most famous line in *Peter Pan*.

Study TIP If it helps, think of **adverbs** as words that **add** to the meaning of **verbs** (but don't misspell the word adverb which has a single 'd'!).

Pronouns

Pronouns stand in the place of nouns. They mean you don't have to keep clumsily repeating the nouns in your sentences. There are several sorts:

- personal
- demonstrative
- possessive
- relative

Note

Demonstrative and possessive pronouns are sometimes referred to as demonstrative or possessive determiners or adjectives.

Study TIP

Take particular care with 'who' and 'whom'.

Whom is used with the accusative, genitive and dative cases (which you may have learnt about in Latin). It follows prepositions such as 'to', 'by', 'of', 'through', 'from' and 'at'. We use it in English when, in a differently structured variation of the sentence, we would use him (not he) or them (not they). Notice that all these words end in **m**.

Note

In modern English 'whom' seems to be dying out – an interesting example of language changing as all languages do continuously. Few newspapers, for example, now use 'whom', choosing instead to use 'who' irrespective of the grammar of the sentence. If you want to capture the voice of an older, well educated person, or a stickler for accuracy, the correct use of 'whom' in your assessment could be a way of doing it. But *never* in any circumstances use 'whom' when the noun it stands for is the subject of the sentence.

- **personal** – I, you, he, she, it, we, they (for the subject of the verb) – me, you, him, her, it, us, them (for the object or 'receiver' of the verb).

  These pronouns take the place of proper or common nouns.

  For example:
  She and **I** went clubbing (subject)
  and
  The paramedic told **them** what to do (object).

- **demonstrative** – This house, that man. Such pronouns often drop the accompanying noun.

  For example:

  This is my house (not This house is my house.)
  or
  This is yours (not This cup/ laptop/ room is yours.)

- **possessive** – his, her, hers, mine, my, their, theirs, our, ours.

  For example:
  This is **her** car. This car is **hers**. That is **his** house. That house is **his**.

- **relative** – who, which, whom, whose, that. These pronouns relate a subordinate clause to the rest of the sentence.

  For example:
  'My grandmother, **whom** you don't know, lives in Ireland.'
  or
  'This is the shop **that** I was telling you about.'
  In these examples the pronouns stand for 'my grandmother' and 'the shop'.

For example:

- This is the teacher from whom I learned DT last year.
  (I learnt it from him.)
- This is the boy with whom I exchanged in France.
  (I exchanged with him.)
- To whom do these football boots belong?
  (Do they belong to him?)
- They are the people from whom I got it.
  (I got it from them.)

Use **who** when, in other circumstances, you would say 'he' or 'they'.

- Who will come to town with me?

  (Will he or she come?)
- We are waiting for Katie who is usually late.

  (She is late.)
- These are the girls who are coming to our house.

  (They are coming.)

Prepositions

Prepositions are used to link nouns or pronouns to some other part of the sentence. They indicate the relationship between two or more things. For instance:

- on
- under
- with

- The information is **on** the computer.

  (Links information and computer. The former is on the latter.)
- **Under** the gravestone lie Heathcliff's remains.

  (Links gravestone and Heathcliff's remains. The latter is under the former.)
- Are you coming **with** us?

  (Potentially links you with us.)

Other prepositions include:

• within	• beneath	• down
• inside	• above	• into
• outside	• around	• with
• over	• up	• at

Many of these words can, as so often in English, also be used to do other jobs in sentences when they are not being prepositions.

Conjunctions

Conjunctions are joining words. They can be used to join sentences to create longer ones or sometimes to hook words together within a sentence.

Common everyday conjunctions include:

• and	• although
• or	• but
• because	• though
• as	• so

For example:

- The prize went jointly to Jessica **and** Alex.
- Felix is going running at the weekend **because** it is his favourite activity.

  (He is going running at the weekend. It is his favourite activity)

Like prepositions, conjunctions are slippery little words. The same words often get into sentences doing other jobs. Look, as ever, at how they are used before you decide what they are.

Articles

'The' is the definite article and refers to something specific.

'A' is the indefinite article.

'An' is a form of the indefinite article used when the next word begins with a vowel.

For example:
- **the** university or **the** river refers to a specific one.

For example:
- **a** giraffe or **a** novel – not specific because we are referring to any giraffe or novel.

For example:
- **an** egg, **an** advocate, **an** unsurprising decision.

Interjections

Although interjections are not strictly speaking a part of speech, it is useful to remind yourself about them here. The word 'interjection' comes from Latin and means forced or thrown between (think of words such as injection, ejection and subjection, which mean, respectively, forced in, forced out and forced under.) In grammar an interjection is a short phrase or single word between sentences. It interrupts the flow and usually expresses strong feelings.

Here are some examples:

- an astonished question such as 'What?' or 'When?'
- a surprised comment such as 'Surely not!', 'Never!' or 'My goodness!'
- an expletive such as 'Damn!', 'Fiddlesticks!', 'Bother!' (and often rather stronger words).

Parts of speech in action

Look at these examples of the parts of speech working together:

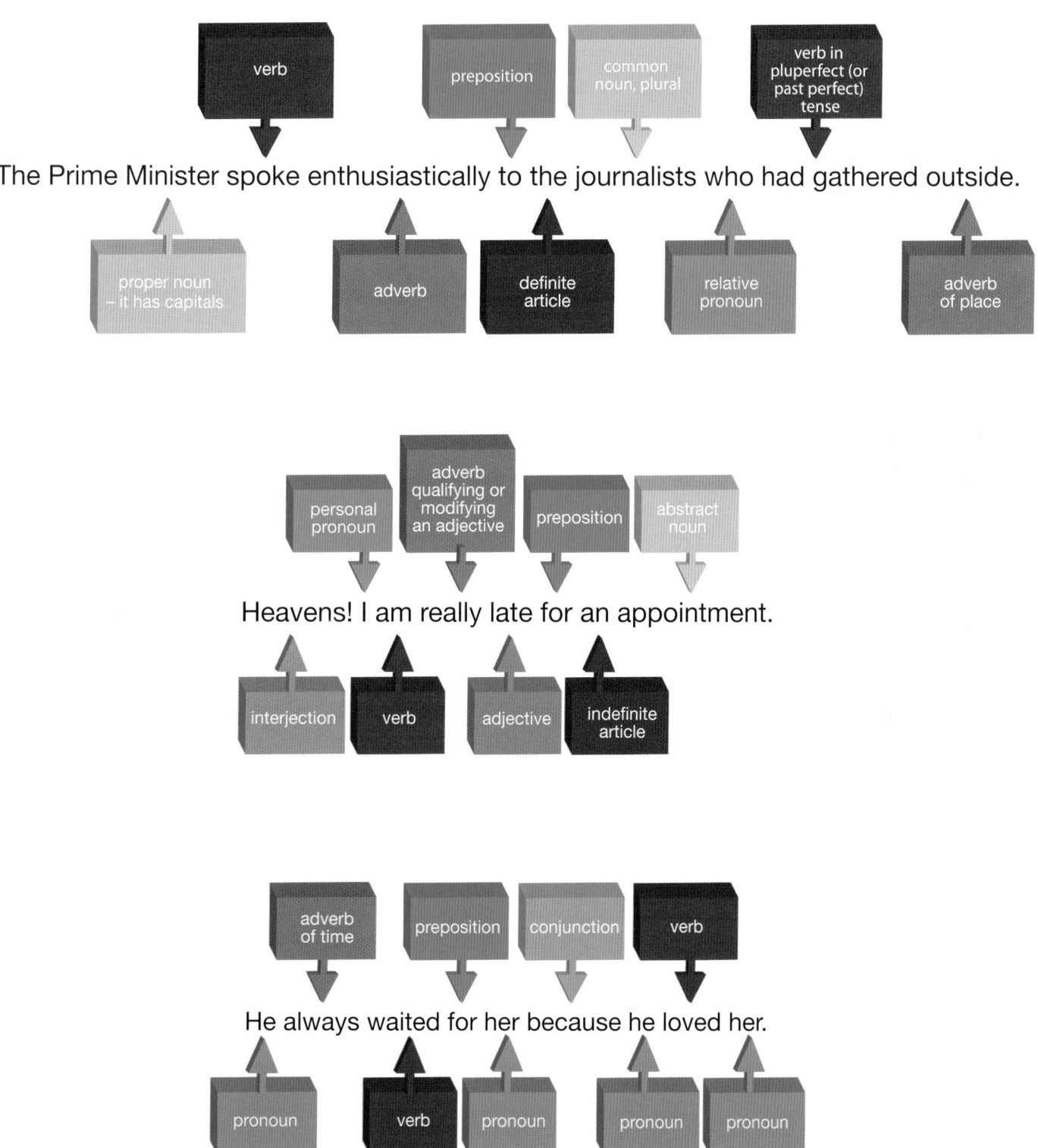

Exercise 15

Some words can be different parts of speech depending on how they are used.

Take the word 'break', for example.

- Why is *break* dancing so popular? (adjective)
- We are all ready for a *break* so it's a good job it's half term next week. (noun)
- I was afraid that I might *break* my ankle the first time I tried trampolining. (verb)

Try using these words as different parts of speech:

- up
- fast
- set
- down

An extra challenge...

- as

Now try to make up your own list.

Then try explaining what you've done to someone who doesn't quite understand it. As any teacher will tell you, the best way of making sure you have grasped something is to teach it to someone else.

Study TIP Read some newspaper and magazine articles and mark-up the different parts of speech.

Agreement of subject and verb

Every sentence has a subject. It may be one word such as 'he' or 'Jessica'. It may be something more complex, such as 'Mrs Eastleigh, our hardworking and helpful Year 11 teacher'. The subject often comes at the beginning of the sentence, but it doesn't have to.

Not far from the subject of any sentence is a verb – the action performed by the subject. The sentence may include other parts too, but a subject and a verb are the basic building bricks.

It is important to make sure that your subject and verb agree. A singular subject needs a singular verb. If the subject is plural, it needs a plural verb.

This is pretty straightforward in sentences such as:

- He walked.
- Jessica wants to change the time of her flute lesson.
- Mrs Eastleigh, our hardworking and helpful Year 11 teacher, deserves a holiday.

But be careful in sentences like this:

- Two sorts of visitor **are** expected.
  (The plural subject 'Two sorts of visitor' needs a plural verb 'are'.)
- What sort of visitor **is** expected?
  (The singular subject 'What sort of visitor' needs a singular verb 'is'.)
- The weather, the miserable surroundings and the poor facilities **were** all responsible for our unsuccessful holiday.
  (The plural subject 'The weather, the miserable surroundings and the poor facilities' need a plural verb 'were'.)
- Everyone **is** here.
  (The singular subject 'everyone' needs a singular verb 'is'.)

Take care with collective nouns. They are singular:

- The Liberal Democrat **Party is** planning its next election campaign.
- The **orchestra is** waiting for its conductor.
- The **flock** of sheep **is** grazed in the top field in summer.

It would, however, be correct to write:

- Liberal Democrat party **members are** planning their next election campaign.
- The **players are** waiting for the orchestra's conductor.
- **Sheep are** grazed in the top field all summer.

Study TIP

Note that these words are all singular and need singular verbs to agree with them:

- anybody
- everybody
- nobody
- anyone

- each
- everyone
- everything
- either

- neither
- none.

For example:

- **Neither** of the accused **was** guilty.
- We made several attempts to trace our ancestry but **none was** successful.
- **Each** of the ten tasks **was** more challenging than the one before.

Clauses and phrases

Clauses and phrases are groups of words within sentences.

A **clause** has a verb of its own. For example:

- A man <u>she **did** not **know**</u> stood on the doorstep.
- We all hoped that <u>when we **left** school</u> we would go to university.
- They stood in the kitchen <u>where most family conferences **were held**</u>.

A clause usually adds extra detail to the main sentence, and if you remove it the sentence should still make sense. Try this with the examples above.

These 'extra' clauses are known as dependent or subordinate clauses because they are pegged on to the main sentences as an extra. The word 'dependent' comes from Latin and means hanging (think of pendant and pendulum). 'Subordinate', also from Latin, means inferior to.

Here are some more examples of dependent (subordinate) clauses:

- She had talked to Mr Chong, <u>who lived on the first floor of our apartment building</u>.
- Their important task was, formally, to hand over the bride to Kegolietile's maternal aunts when they <u>approached the yard at sunset</u>.
- The visitors' book, <u>which was kept at the college reception</u>, provided all the evidence <u>the police needed</u>.

A **phrase** is two or more words used together in a sentence. It can be a word group of almost any shape, for example:

- We followed him <u>through the park</u> until we reached the main road.
- They had eaten dinner <u>earlier that evening</u>.
- <u>Given the choice</u>, I like fantasy stories best.
- Freddie set out <u>wearing his cycling helmet</u>.

Examiner's TIP

Good sentences consist of varying patterns of clauses and phrases woven together. Aim for this in all your writing and look carefully at how writers use clauses and phrases when you are analysing texts.

The following two pages list and explain ten important mistakes to avoid if you want to achieve A* in your assessments.

Ten mistakes to avoid

1 Don't confuse the pronouns **I** and **me** when they are used in a sentence with another person. 'I' is usually the subject in the sentence or clause and 'me' is the object (direct or indirect). If in doubt, take the other person out of the sentence to see what you would write if you were using the pronoun on its own. The pronoun remains the same when you put the other person back in. So you should write:

- Osama and I played squash.
  (You wouldn't write 'Me played squash') ✗
- She gave him and me a hard time.
  (You wouldn't write 'She gave I a hard time') ✗
- That's all for today from him and me.
  (You wouldn't write 'That's all for today from I') ✗
- 'Me and Tommy went to the cinema' is always wrong. ✗

2 Never use **himself, herself** or **myself** as the subject of a sentence. The following are always wrong:

- Mr Ethelbert and myself have ... ✗
- Myself and Mr Ethelbert have ... ✗
- Myself will ... ✗

3 Be careful with **too**, **to** and **two**.

- I am **too** old to wear plaits with ribbons. (too much of something)
- We both ate **two** jam doughnuts. (number)
- My mother often has **to** go **to** the council offices in town. (all other uses including part of a verb or a preposition)

Learn this sentence to help you remember:

- Two cats, too curious for their own good, ran to the cupboard to look inside.

4 Learn the difference between **all ready** and **already**.

- Are we **all ready** to go?

('Ready' is an adjective telling you more about 'we'. 'All' is a separate adverb telling you more about 'ready'. This sentence means 'Are all of us ready to go?')

- He has arrived **already**.

('Already' is an adverb. Here it means 'in good time' or 'ahead of the time when he might have been expected'.)

5 Spell **all right** correctly. For formal writing it is two separate words, 'all' and 'right'. Alright is now acceptable in informal writing. Remember that **thank you** is also two words. So is **a lot**, and **in spite of** is three separate words.

6 Be careful with **less**, **few** and **fewer**.

Less refers to quantity. For example:

- less salt
- less rainfall
- less hope.

Fewer or few refer to number. For example:

- fewer eggs
- few people
- few schools.

A quick way of remembering this is that if it's something you can count (eggs, people, houses) it is 'few' or 'fewer'. If you can't count whatever it is, use 'less'.

(One or two British supermarkets have notices up that read 'Baskets containing fewer than eight items' – which is correct. Several other supermarkets get this wrong.)

7 Learn the difference between the three verbs **to lie** (with its two meanings) and **to lay**.

To lie means either to put oneself in a horizontal position or to tell untruths.

The past tense for the first meaning is 'lay', for example:

- I **lay** on the grass all day yesterday.

or 'have lain', for example:

- I **have lain** on the grass all morning and now it's time for lunch.

You should also write:

- On Sundays (if you're lucky) you might enjoy a lie-in.

The untruth sense is easier. The past tense is 'lied' or 'have lied', for example:

- I **lied** to him yesterday because I **have** always **lied** to him.

To lay is used when the person or thing carrying out the action (the verb's subject) is doing something to something else. (This is known as a transitive verb.)

So, for example:

- You can **lay** eggs (if you are a hen), bricks, carpets and tables.

The past tense is 'laid' or 'have laid', for example:

- These are new-**laid** eggs.
- They have **laid** the table.

8 Be sure to put the word **only** in the correct place in a sentence. Getting it wrong (as many people do) changes the meaning. Study these examples:

- **Only** we saw the play that afternoon.
  (No one else saw it.)
- We saw **only** the play that afternoon.
  (We didn't see anything else.)
- We **only** saw the play that afternoon.
  (We didn't, for example, read it or rehearse it.)
- We saw the play **only** that afternoon.

(We had seen it very recently, or we didn't see the play on any other occasion, at another time or a second time.)

Take care with other adverbs such as **even**, **always** and **often** too. These two sentences do not mean quite the same thing:

- It seemed strange even to us.
- It even seemed strange to us.

Attention to such precision will improve the quality of your writing and help to get you more marks in your assessments.

9 Learn the different spellings of the noun and verb forms of certain words.

Practice is a noun.

- I must do some clarinet practice.
- Practice is important if you want to improve your tennis.
- Dr Ahmed's medical practice covered three villages.

Sometimes it becomes an adjective, for example:

- The practice rooms are at the back of the music block.
- Sunday morning is practice time for musical instruments in our house.

Practise is a verb:

- I must practise for my Spanish oral assessment.
- Practise your golf strokes if you want to improve.
- Dr Kai practises in three villages.

Use **advice** and **advise** to help you remember this. They are helpful because they sound different. Say aloud:

- Let me give you some advice. (noun)
- We could try the advice centre. (adjective)
- I advise you to start revising now. (verb)
- She advised me to talk to you. (verb)

Licence/license and **prophecy/prophesy** follow the same pattern.

Note that in American English these words are always spelled with a 'c' even when they are verbs.

10 Remember that a phrase or clause used before the subject of a sentence is linked to that subject. This will help you to avoid writing sentences that are nonsense or confusing. For example:

- Being a tiring day, I decided not to go out again. ✗

This is nonsense. I am not a tiring day! You should write one of the following:

- It had been a tiring day so I decided not to go out again.
- I decided not to go out again because it had been a tiring day.

- Knowing he was about to leave, Henry stopped talking and listened to Mr Todd. ✗

This is confusing. Who is about to leave? Henry? Mr Todd? You should write, for example:

- Henry stopped talking and listened to Mr Todd who was about to leave.

Practise other ways of expressing this sentence so that it says what it means.

Punctuation

This Section finishes with a summary of the most important uses of the main punctuation marks used in English. Ensure that you know how to use these as poor punctuation will cost you marks in your assessments.

Full stops

Every sentence must end with a full stop (.) Or, if appropriate, with a question mark (?) or exclamation mark (!), both of which include a full stop.

Never end a sentence with a comma. Remember that some sentences can be very short and short sentences often make for good writing.

Study the extract opposite, from George Orwell's novel *Animal Farm*, for correct use of the full stop as a sentence ending. Notice how short some of the sentences are.

November came, with raging south-west winds. Building had to stop because it was now too wet to mix the cement. Finally there came a night when the gale was so violent that the farm buildings rocked on their foundations and several tiles were blown off the roof of the barn. The hens woke up squawking with terror because they had all dreamed simultaneously of hearing a gun go off in the distance. In the morning the animals came out of their stalls to find that the flagstaff had blown down and an elm tree at the foot of the orchard had been plucked up like a radish. They had just noticed this when a cry of despair broke from every animal's throat. A terrible sight met their eyes. The windmill was in ruins.

From *Animal Farm* by George Orwell (1945)

Use a **question mark** if a question is being asked. For example:

- How far is it to Edinburgh?
- Will it take long to get there?

Use an **exclamation mark** if you want to turn something you've written into a joke or to make an exclamation dramatic. For example:

- Help!
- Oh my God!
- Shiver my timbers!

Generally it is bad style, and lazy, to use exclamation marks other than very occasionally. If your choice of words is strong enough, exclamation marks are usually unnecessary. Think how rarely you see them in newspapers, information books or in good novels (except sometimes in dialogue).

Examiner's TIP

Never use more than one exclamation mark at a time in an assessment.

Commas

Commas are used to mark a natural break in a sentence or to separate one part of a sentence from another. For example:

- Come and sit with us, Rani.
- Please, park your car over there.
- Always ready for a joke, my Dad wore a blonde wig to his office Christmas party.

They are also used to separate items in a list within a sentence. Note that you do not use a comma before the 'and'. For example:

- Pasta, pizza, pesto and pinenuts are my favourite Italian foods.
- I've read several war poems by Wilfred Owen, two by Siegfried Sassoon, one by Robert Graves, another by Rupert Brooke and some extracts from David Jones's *In Parenthesis*.
- Worried, nervous and frightened, Adam drew his phone from his pocket.

Commas are also used in pairs to separate an aside from the main thrust of the sentence. For example:

- It is unlikely, it would seem, to happen.
- Mary Glover, a maths professor, told the group about studying her subject at university.
- Ashley, who transferred to our school only last year, is the finest goalkeeper the first eleven has ever had.

Colons

The colon (:) means 'as follows'. It is used to introduce a list or to announce and draw attention to a statement. For instance, it is used throughout this book to introduce a point or example. It is sometimes used instead of a comma to introduce spoken words. For example:

- In the supermarket the couple bought these items: fruit, vegetables, beer, bread and several sorts of cheese.
- We were given the following advice: never jump into water wearing jeans because they absorb water, become heavy and will drag you down.
- This is the point: we cannot all go so some of us must agree to opt out.
- To our dismay the station public address system suddenly announced: 'the 11.30 train to London has been cancelled owing to an obstruction on the line and we don't know when it will be cleared.'
- These people attended the meeting: Peter Ellison, Amaka Amada, Sylvia Smith, Florence Johnson and Mark Headley.

Examiner's TIP

The use of the colon makes for a crisp, quite formal style.

In British English the colon is not usually followed by a capital letter unless the word is a proper noun or an acronym, such as NATO. Note, however, that in American English, which we are very used to seeing, the rules are different and there is often a capital letter after a colon.

Semicolons

The semicolon (;) is stronger than a comma but weaker than a full stop. It has two main uses:

1. It can divide two related statements, each of which could – if the writer chose – be a sentence in its own right. It is not followed by a capital letter and links the two statements. For example:

- The reasonable person adapts himself to the world; the unreasonable one persists in trying to adapt the world to himself.
- Tim Rice is a lyricist; Seamus Heaney is a poet.
- Eat drink and be merry; tomorrow we die.

You could, of course, in each of these examples replace the semicolon with a conjunction such as 'but', 'while' or 'for' to create one long sentence but it might have less impact. You need to be aware of the effect on style such choices make.

2. It can be used in a complex sentence where you need commas to punctuate the items within the semicolons, giving you this sort of pattern:

 ----; ----, ----; ----, ----, ----; ----, ---- and ----.
For example:

Note
- like the colon, the semicolon is not followed by a capital letter unless the word after the semicolon is a proper noun or an acronym
- in a list, as in simple lists separated by commas, you do not need a semicolon before the final 'and'.

There were white-tusked wild males, with fallen leaves and nuts and twigs lying in the folds of their necks and the folds of their ears; fat, slow-footed she-elephants, with restless little pinky-black calves only three or four feet high running under their stomachs; young elephants with tusks just beginning to show, and very proud of them; lanky, scraggy old-maid elephants, with their hollow, anxious faces and trunks like rough bark; savage old bull elephants, scarred from shoulder to flank with great weals and cuts of bygone fights and the caked dirt of their solitary mud-baths drooping from their shoulders and there was one with a broken tusk and the marks of the full-stroke, the terrible drawing scrape of a tiger's claws on his side.

source unknown

Examiner's TIP The use of the semi-colon makes for a fluid style.

Capital letters

Every sentence *must* begin with a capital (upper case) letter.

Sometimes handwriting makes it difficult to tell whether a letter is lower or upper case (small or capital). Make sure your writing is not guilty of this. If you don't, the examiner will assume that you are making punctuation errors.

Most capital letters are larger than the other letters in a word – make the distinction clearly, especially when the two forms are the same, or similar, shape such as Ss, Oo or Kk.

Many are a different shape such as Bb or Dd. Some like Pp and Jj have a different position on the page. Pay attention to this so that the examiner does not think you are misusing capital letters. If it looks to someone who is unfamiliar with your writing as though you are failing to begin sentences and proper nouns with capitals you will lose marks.

You also need a capital letter for proper nouns (names), for example:

- Ella Thompson, Bridgetown Secondary School, Cardiff, River Tweed, Superdrug

At the beginning of most lines of poetry, for example:

- 'Between my finger and my thumb
  The squat pen rests; snug as a gun.'

For the first word inside inverted commas, for example:

- Felicia said, 'And I'll come too,' when she saw us getting ready.

For initials and acronyms, for example:

- AIDS, NSPCC, GCSE.

Speech marks

Also sometimes called inverted commas or quotation marks (" " or ' '), speech marks always work in pairs. They separate a group of spoken or quoted words from the rest of the sentence.

Note the following rules:

- A capital letter is used each time speech marks are opened unless the speaker is in the middle of a sentence. For example:

  Mr Ferguson said 'We must leave immediately.'

  'I really think,' argued his daughter, 'that we should wait for Mum.'

- A comma is usually used at the end of the spoken words inside the speech marks before the writer explains who is speaking. For example:

  'That's right,' said Jack.

  'I think that's interesting,' observed Leila.

- If what is said ends with a question mark or exclamation mark, this goes inside the speech marks. If the writer goes on to explain who is speaking, this starts with a lower case letter. For example:

  'Are you telling me the truth?' asked Max.

  'Wow!' murmured Aileen.

- A new paragraph begins each time a different character speaks.

Study these pieces of dialogue as a way of revising speech marks:

Suddenly I heard the old tailor's voice rumbling in the dark.

'Why did you stop?'

'Pardon me!' I exclaimed. 'I thought you were asleep.'

'By no means. I've been listening all the time. I like your story.'

'I'm too tired to go on.'

'Well, try to keep it up just a little longer,' the old tailor pleaded.

'All right, just a little while,' I said. 'Do you remember where I left off?'

From *Balzac and the Little Chinese Seamstress* by Dai Sijie (2001)

I cannot believe,' said Silas, 'that you could have been so ... so stupid. Everything I told you about this side of invisibility. And now you've become the talk of the school?'

'Well what did you want me to do?'

'Not this,' said Silas. 'It's not like olden times. They can keep track of you, Bod. They can find you.'

From *The Graveyard Book* by Neil Gaiman (2008)

 Examiner's **TIP**

It doesn't matter whether you use single speech marks (' ') or doubles (" ") but you must be consistent.

If you need to use speech marks within a passage that is already in speech marks, use the type that you have not already used. This gives one or other of the following patterns:

- 'Bla bla "bla bla" bla bla.'
- "Bla bla 'bla bla' bla bla."

Study this example:

'Why winter? Just oak.'

'No, not just oak. Winter oak, that's the noun.'

'Sit down, Savushkin. This is what happens when you are late. "Oak" is a noun and we have not yet come to what "winter" would be. Kindly come and see me in the staff-room during break.'

From 'The Winter Oak' by Yuri Nagibin (1955) translated from Russian by H Goscilo (1986)

Apostrophes

The apostrophe (') has two uses. It shows:

- possession
- that letters have been missed out (omission).

A. Possession

When the possessor is singular the apostrophe goes before the s:

- Felicia's chair is the chair possessed by Felicia (one person – singular).
- A year's work is the work connected with, or possessed by, the year (one year – singular).

When the possessor noun is plural the apostrophe (usually) goes after the s:

- The boys' toilet is the toilet used, or possessed by, the boys (more than one boy – plural).
- Three days' practice is practice lasting, or possessed by, three days (more than one day – plural).

Take care with words that already end in s or ss in their singular or plural form. Exactly the same rules apply:

- The actress's costume (singular)
- Three princesses' travel arrangements (plural)
- The albatrosses' nesting site (plural)
- Charles Dickens's first novel (singular)
- Mrs Williams's class (singular)
- King Charles's reign (singular)

Note that the handful of plural nouns that do not end in s – such as men and women – behave as if they were singular and take an apostrophe before the s when they are possessive. For example:

- women's health
- children's books.

B. Omission

The apostrophe also stands in place of missing letters in contractions of words such as:

- didn't (did not)
- o'clock (of the clock)
- I'm (I am)
- P'borough (Peterborough – as on road signs)
- it's (it is or it has)
- here's (here is)

Be particularly careful with **its** which means **of it** and **it's** which means **it is** or **it has**.

Learn this sentence to help you remember:

- **It's** a nuisance that our car has failed **its** MOT.

Remember that an s at the end of a word usually indicates a plural noun (three students, four motorbikes, two glasses, etc.) or part of a verb (he argues, she swims, Isabella shouts, Oliver calculates).

None of these need an apostrophe. For example:

- Most of the pupils in classes nine, ten and eleven enjoy basketball lessons but Lucas Jones says he prefers racquet sports.

Historical Note

The apostrophe was originally used only to indicate a missing letter

It's cold = It is cold

It is now also used to show possession

Paul's hat = the hat of Paul

This is because, in Old English, possession was indicated by the suffix (or ending) –es

Paules book = the book of Paul

The 'es' ending was pronounced as a separate syllable, but as the spoken language changed people stopped pronouncing the 'e' and the two syllable word Paul-es became the one syllable word Pauls.

An apostrophe was used to show the missing e. Thus we get Paul's.

That is why we now use apostrophes to show possession. Understanding this might help you to use apostrophes correctly.

Examiner's TIP

Remember that far more words do *not* need an apostrophe than need one. Do your best to learn how the apostrophe is used and get it right in your exam. But if you are in doubt, leave it out as you will make fewer mistakes that way.

Spelling Accurately

Spellings

This book concludes with a section of the most commonly misspelt words in the English language. They have been split up so you can concentrate on one column at a time, only moving on once you are confident you can spell all the words in a column correctly.

The spellings do not have to be learnt in order, but it is important that you are able to spell accurately in your assessments. Therefore make learning these words, just one or two each day perhaps, a crucial part of your GCSE/IGCSE work. Learn the words by writing them down. Don't spell them aloud as this is a different skill (and a more difficult one for most people). In your assessments and exams you will need to write the words so concentrate on that. Once you have really mastered a particular word you are unlikely ever to have a problem with it again. And it usually takes only a minute or two's concentration.

 Examiners expect to see accurate spelling from A* candidates and avoiding using a word in an exam because you can't spell it is a very lazy solution and limits your vocabulary. It is much better to spend a little time learning any spellings you don't know. You will then be able to use these words with confidence in all your exam subjects as well as English.

absence	aerial	argument
accelerate	agreeable	assassinate
access	alcohol	assistant
accommodation	allege	association
achieve	analyse	attachment
acquiesce	anxious	author
across	appal	autumn
address	appalling	auxiliary
advantageous	arctic	awkward

basically	caricature	comparative
beautiful	catarrh	comparison
beginning	ceiling	conceit
benefited	cemetery	condemn
biscuit	changeable	conscience
boisterous	commemorate	conscientious
business	commit	conscious
calendar	committed	consensus
campaign	committee	

coolly	disappear	disaster
correspondence	disappoint	disastrous
corroborate	desirable	disillusioned
cynicism	despair	dissatisfy
deceit	deteriorate	drunkenness
deceive	development	duly
definitely	diarrhoea	ecstasy
desiccated	dilemma	eerie

eighth	extraordinary	fulfil
eligible	exuberant	gauge
embarrass	feasible	goddess
exaggerate	February	government
exceed	fiery	grammatical
except	fluorescent	guarantee
excessive	foreign	guard
excitement	forfeit	
exhilaration	forty	

handkerchief	hypocrisy	insistent
harass	illegibly	install
height	immediate	instalment
hindrance	imminent	intellectual
holiday	incidentally	irrelevant
humorous	independent	irresistible
humour	indispensable	irreverent
hygiene	innocence	irritable

install	laboratory	maintenance
instalment	leisure	manageable
jealousy	liaison	manoeuvring
jeopardy	library	marriageable
jewellery	likeable	mathematician
keenness	likelihood	Mediterranean
knowledge	lovable	miniature
knowledgeable	maintain	miscellaneous

mischief	negotiate	occurring
mischievous	neighbour	omission
misspelling	niece	overrule
misspelt	ninety	parallel
murmur	noticeable	paralleled
murmuring	nuisance	paralyse
necessarily	occasionally	pastime
necessary	occur	permissible
negligent	occurrence	

perseverance	predictable	publicly
persistent	prejudice	pursue
picnic	privilege	quarrel
picnicking	procedure	quarrelling
playwright	proceed	queue
poisonous	profession	quietly
possession	pronounce	receipt
precede	pronunciation	receive
predecessor	psychiatrist	recommend

refer	rhythm	separate
referee	ridiculous	sergeant
reference	rogue	siege
referring	rouge	silhouette
religious	sacrilegious	sincerely
reminiscence	satellite	solemn
repetition	scissors	soliloquies
restaurant	secretarial	soliloquy
rhyme	secretary	

subtlety	through	vehicle
subtly	tranquil	vengeance
succeed	tranquillity	veterinary
success	transfer	vicious
supersede	transference	vigorous
symmetry	transferring	weird
technique	truly	wholly
temporary	tyranny	wilfully
tendency	tyrant	witticism
theatre	undoubtedly	woollen
theatrical	unnecessary	yacht
thorough	vacuum	yield